Terence Wilson gives us a peek into the personal struggle and triumph of a child growing up and dealing with the reality of living life without a father. This book is an excellent source on how to overcome in a world where the absence of a father is an epidemic. In this fatherless generation, this book is a ray of inspiration, encouragement, and healing. *In Search of a Father* is a must read for anyone who is affected by the reality of divorce.

Wayne T. Jackson
Bishop and Senior Pastor
Great Faith International Ministries, Detroit, MI

Fatherless families are America's single largest source of crime and poverty. Terrence Wilson's resilience and self-motivation is an inspiration to anyone in search of a father. Restoring responsible fatherhood is a critical priority achieved by responding to the father heart of God. *In Search of a Father,* is a timely book for a desperate generation.

Dr. Jamal Harrison Bryant
Senior Pastor, Empowerment Temple
Baltimore, MD

Much of what is wrong with our society today is the direct result of absentee fathers. So many of our children are dying and have felt a *dying for hunger* for their fathers. They're hungry for Daddy's covering, care, training, and touch. But Daddy has been absent. He's not there.

In his book *In Search of a Father,* Terrence Wilson has touched on a painful and challenging issue that impacts the nation at large. You should be encouraged to read this in your Bible groups, and study groups. Let's not hide, but face the issue and allow God to turn the *hearts of the children to their fathers.*

Bishop Donald Hilliard
Senior Pastor, Cathedral International
Perth Amboy, NJ

In Search of a Father will help anyone who has not had a father in order to "locate themselves" in God. Reading this book is empowering, and right on time! Men, quit being hoodwinked by the devil; stand up and take your rightful place in the Kingdom! You are made in HIS image! Know it, speak it, live it! This book will show you how.

Ty Adams
Author of *Single, Saved and Still Having Sex*
Founder & Evangelist, Heaven Enterprises

Terrence Wilson is a man who grew up without his father, yet always yearned for the Father's touch. In his book, Terrence explores the value one can receive about fathering from the Father who created all fathers. This is a *must read*, not only for men who grew up fatherless, but this book can also shine some light for the women who have to deal with men who have been fatherless.

Anthony Shannon
Senior Pastor, Beyond the Veil International Ministries
Berkley, MI

To Truth Bookstore,
May God continue to prosper you!!!

[signature]

2-2-12

Behold, I will send you Elijah the prophet before the coming of the great and dreadful day of the LORD:
And he shall turn the heart of the fathers to the children, and the heart of the children to their fathers, lest I come and smite the earth with a curse.

Malachi 4: 5, 6

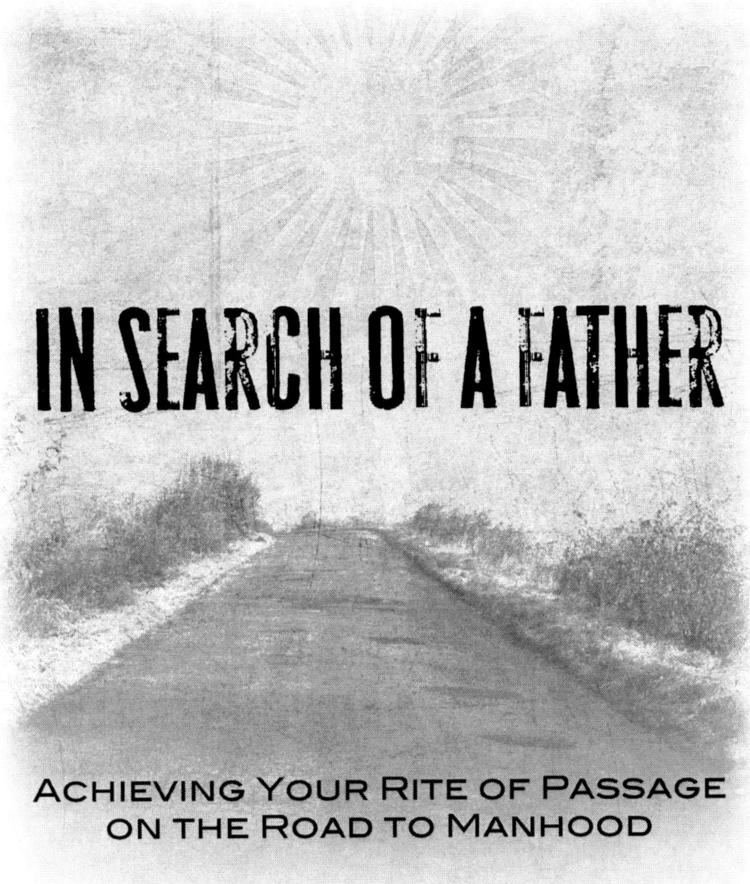

IN SEARCH OF A FATHER

ACHIEVING YOUR RITE OF PASSAGE ON THE ROAD TO MANHOOD

TERRENCE WILSON

Alachua, Florida 32615

Bridge-Logos
Alachua, FL 32615 USA

In Search of a Father
by Terrence Wilson

Edited by Beverlee Chadwick

Copyright ©2010 by Bridge-Logos

All rights reserved. Under International Copyright Law, no part of this publication may be reproduced, stored, or transmitted by any means—electronic, mechanical, photographic (photocopy), recording, or otherwise—without written permission from the Publisher.

Printed in the United States of America.

Library of Congress Catalog Card Number: pending
International Standard Book Number: 978-0-88270-996-3

Scripture quotations are taken from the *King James Version* of the Bible unless otherwise indicated.

Dedication

First and foremost, I dedicate this book to God, my heavenly Father, for all of the many blessings He has bestowed upon me. I will forever love you.

I dedicate this book to my mother who was always there for me, and made sure that all my needs were provided for; even if hers were not. Your blessing is soon to come.

I also dedicate this book to all the fathers who have provided a loving and secure household for their families. May the blessing of God be upon you and your household.

I dedicate this book to all who may feel like they are failing, but want to overcome. With Christ, you *will* make it.

Psalm 118:6 states: *The LORD is on my side; I will not fear: what can man do unto me?*

A Memo from My Dad

When I first obtained a copy of this book, I became offended. How could my son write such bad things about his father? The answer was simple: "I wasn't a father to him." Yes, I started out as a father; however, I lost focus on his needs because of my own selfishness.

It's easy to have a pity party and think only about yourself—about how you were raised, the training you did not receive because your father wasn't there. It was easy to talk about the hurt I had encountered, but it is easier to change. After reviewing the contents closer, I realized I had no right to be offended for what I created.

I owed my son an apology, for I had failed to be a real father to him. This book was rewarding and refreshing to me, for it truly became an eye-opener. First, it showed me material things are nice, but mean nothing if you don't provide true love and support. As I listened, with opened heart to what TJ conveyed, I began to see my dreams unfold in my son. The desires I had as a young man [and did not tell him] were now coming to fruition through my son.

I strongly encourage fathers all over (present and absent) to obtain a copy of *In Search of a Father*. I want them to understand how my son felt, and perhaps they will not make the same mistake I did in not being a vital piece in the up bringing of our sons. Remember, *your son is a reflection of you*.

TJ, thanks for sharing your intimate feelings with me. As well, I applaud your gallant efforts in attempting to provide healing to the many young men and fathers who feel the same way you felt.

—Dad

Foreword

Fathers are not obsolete. This is a primary conclusion from *In Search of a Father*. It is clearly articulated that Fathers are necessary, fundamental, and essential for positive personal development especially as it relates to growing into manhood.

God prophesied that Ishmael would be "a wild man; his hand shall be against every man, and every man's hand shall be against him" (Gen. 16:12). Judges 11:3, describes Jephthah as one who "fled from his brethren, dwelt in the land of Tob, and there were gathered vain men to Jephthah, and went out with him." *The New Living Translation* says Jephthah "soon had a band of worthless rebels following him." *The Message Translation* of this same verse says "some riffraff joined him and went around with him." So, Ishmael was "wild man" and Jephthah was a "thug and gang banger." The one thing that Ishmael and Jephthah had in common was that they were estranged from their fathers. Consequently they became "wild," and hung out with the wrong people —a common consequence of "fatherlessness."

No, despite the increase in single parents households, lesbian couples, and even those of us who have become successful despite not having them with us, *fathers* are neither obsolete, nor dispensable. Just about every social ill that we can name has some correlation with, if not causation by, fatherlessness; teenage pregnancy; high school drop out rates; crime; juvenile delinquency; poverty; alcohol; and drug abuse, the list goes on and on. The issue of "fatherlessness" is so dear to God that He commands us to "defend the poor and fatherless" (Ps. 82:3). God commanded his people to leave food for the "fatherless" (Deut. 14:29; Deut. 24:19). God is described in the Scriptures as a "Helper of the fatherless" (Ps. 10:14), and a "Reliever" of the fatherless (Ps. 146:9). In the New Testament, James reminded the early church that the religion would be demonstrated when they "visit the fatherless" (James 1:27).

Since the issue of absentee fathers (for whatever reason) is a big deal to God, shouldn't it be a big deal to us? If you are or were fortunate enough to be raised in a Christian home by a godly father and mother, you have been blessed indeed. However, that is not the testimony of many people throughout America or the world. The issue is compounded more within African-American families. If you have been one of the fortunate ones to have the privilege of being raised in a two-parent family with a godly father, you may not realize the gaps, deficits and plight of those who have not been blessed to share your experience.

Get ready to open your heart, soul, and mind to feel the pain of Terrence Wilson as he shares he journey In Search of a Father. But don't stop there, rejoice with him as he discovers intimacy with God the father who makes up the difference and caused him to move from victim to victor. You too will rejoice in the privilege of knowing God as "Abba father."

Terrence Wilson has conquered his pain and turned it into gain for the benefit of the fatherless. He shares the deeper issues resulting from absentee fathers and helps us reconcile the feelings and thoughts that very few of us dare to acknowledge or share. I had the privilege of having raised four children: three boys and a girl in a Christian marriage with the same women for over 25 years. Our children are the fruit of our labor—college students and graduates, serving the Lord and raising a new generation of godly seed. This book will help you to evaluate your role as a parent to make sure that you are not only teaching but imparting the principles necessary to perpetuate the blessing of the Lord from generation to generation.

Dr. Herbert Bailey
Senior Pastor, Right Direction Christian Center
Columbia, SC

Contents

My Testimony 1

Chapter 1—A Father in the Eyes of His Son 7

Chapter 2—A Son in the Eyes of the Father. 25

Chapter 3—Created in the Image of My Natural Father. . .41

Chapter 4—Re-Created in the Image of My

    Heavenly Father. 59

Chapter 5—Masking It 85

Chapter 6—Learning to Live in Power 105

Chapter 7—Living in Love & Forgiveness 123

Chapter 8—A Mother's Love 141

Chapter 9—We Still Need Our Fathers. 155

Special Invitation 171

Special Acknowledgements. 173

Only God Knows

No one knows my struggles,
No one can see my troubles,
They only see my glory.
Yet and still, I press
To pass this test
And this is my story.
I live this life day-by-day,
Fighting to walk the straight and narrow way.
Stumbling along this path called life,
I wish I may, I wish I might,
Bring an end to this everlasting fight.
At times I have fallen flat on my face,
Even as I pace myself to run this Christian race
On my way to a place I've never been before.
So I walk through a door prepared just for me.
My life has been blessed
Because His glory has been manifested.
He's given me wings to fly
So I soar high through the sky,
And as I float through the clouds,
My mind wonders back to where
I came from and the trials
I've faced.
And I wonder, "How in the world
Did I arrive at this place?"
Only God knows.

My Testimony

It has been a long journey to the completion of this book. It has been trying and pressing, but well worth it. I began writing this book in South Carolina in 1999, however, due to time and other obligations I did not finish it. Then in the year 2000, I moved to Detroit, Michigan. I had every intention of getting back to it as soon as I became settled in my new surroundings. Needless to say, I did not.

As time went on, I encountered some trials and tribulations that really affected me spiritually, emotionally, and physically. It affected me spiritually from the standpoint that I did not want to pursue ministry any longer. I was fed up and just wanted to go into hiding; disappear from the scene. I could not see God anywhere in my situation and was thinking that, maybe, I missed it.

It affected me emotionally in that I began to waver in many of my decisions. I would start doing something and later change my mind because it did not feel right. It felt right when I started doing it but my feelings changed. Due to a traumatic experience, I became real emotional, only making decisions that would make me feel like I had peace. From that experience, I have learned to never let my emotions or people influence me when making a decision. Many times people will tell you what they think you should do because it is what they want you to do, not because it is best for you. It is a shame but sometimes you have to limit the amount of influence a person has over you, or you will never be you.

It affected me physically in that my body became fatigued and worn. My body also suffered affects from a spiritual attack by a demonic force. One time when I was driving in my car, I was attacked with such demonic force that a burst of air seemed to blow out of the left side of my heart and up the side of my face causing me to be paralyzed for a few seconds. I went to the emergency room and after observing me for several hours they could not find out what the problem was. The only thing they came up with was that I was on cocaine because of my rapid heart rate and had me take a blood test because they did not believe me when I denied it. It is only by the grace of God I am alive today.

At the same time, I was stretching myself beyond my natural limits by working full time , going to school full time, and being a single man I did all my cooking, cleaning and other chores. I was over nine hundred miles from the closest relative, so basically I was on my own, and my nature and character being what they were, I was used to being the strong one for everyone else, so I kept my troubles to myself because I had to show strength for others. It was in my nature and character. This trait could be seen as good for certain things, but you always need an outlet, someone to whom you can talk to who can be objective. I knew some people I could talk to, but they were in South Carolina and I was in Detroit.

In the meantime, the pressure on me built even more as other people were calling me about their problems and issues. I wanted to be there for them, and not wanting to disappoint them, I was always ready to listen to them. However, I remember thinking to myself as I lay cradled on my couch, *where is my shoulder to cry on?* Finally, one day I remember saying, "*I want my daddy.*" At twenty-five years of age, I was reaching for a support figure to fall back on, but he was not there. "*Why me?*" I cried out to God. I was frustrated, angry, bitter, and most of all, confused. I was at a breaking point.

My Testimony

However, I was reminded of when Paul was looking to escape the pressure of dealing with a thorn in his flesh, which was the messenger of Satan sent to buffet him. After repeatedly seeking God to remove the thorn, God tells him *"My grace is sufficient for you, for my power is made perfect in weakness"* (1 Corinthians 12:7-9. Many times we seek to run from our circumstances when God commands us to overcome them. At that point in time, I began to gather strength in the Word of God. I also decided that not only would I make it, but that I would reach back my hand to help all who came from the same situation I did. I was determined that my victory over this trial would not just be mine alone: I was not coming out by myself.

When Jesus Christ arose from the grave, He was not alone. Many of the saints that had died arose (Matthew 27: 52, 53) and when He comes back millions more will rise as well. He not only gained victory over death in His situation, He gained victory over the grave in my situation too. And that, my friend, is my purpose for writing this book. I know that there are many young people, as well as older, who have battled with something similar. Some are struggling to make it. Some are waning in the balances. Some have given up completely.

On October 13, 2002, I was driving home from a boy's home detention center and I heard a voice whisper in my ear, *In Search of a Father*. I thought to myself, *I'll write a book called In Search of a Father: what a good idea*. Immediately, when I got home I began to gather different material that I already had. In going through it, I found written as the title of the book I started in 1999, *In Search of a Father*.

I knew then I was destined to write this book.

The Holy Ghost, who dwells on the inside of me, brought back to my remembrance what Jesus told me to do back in 1999 and it was now the time to complete it (John 14:26). God had started a good work in me and He was about to finish it. My message is very clear. There is hope and His name is Jesus

Christ. Yet, I have learned it is we who have to cleave unto the hope of Christ.

My prayer is that this book will cause men to turn their hearts back towards their families: to help them see and understand the importance of the role they play in the lives of their wives and children. Men must begin to accept their roles and responsibilities in the family by knowing that this life is no longer just about them.

You are more important than you know and your relevance to your family can never be understated. It does not matter if you are single, freshly married, or on the brink of divorce, your impact on your family is still a necessity. So please believe me when I say this, "We (your family) need(s) you."

In Search of a Father

Searching for someone to help share this burden
I've borne since the age of five as I survive
Second by second.

Someone to be there
to whom I can carry my care
Instead of wearing myself out
having to fight each bout
Blow-by-blow.

I need an open ear, someone to hear
My deepest thoughts, my inner most secrets,
And reply with words of wisdom.
Someone to help me achieve my heart's desire,
And when I'm down to
Take me higher.

Someone to shield me from the elements of death;
To whom I can retreat when my fears
Try to overcome me.

In whose presence, I can allow tears to fill my eyes,
Without the feeling of my manhood being despised
When the stress begins to get to me.
I am in search of a father.

Chapter 1

A Father in the Eyes of His Son

The Creator of My World

The best place for me to start is to explain my first relationship with my father. Even though short-lived, it was the most critical relationship I have ever had. I loved him. He was my father, and I was proud to be his son. Just the short time period that we shared helped me to formulate what things I liked, and what things I did not. What was acceptable, and what was not.

A child's glory comes from their father (Proverbs 17:6). That word glory denotes honor, splendor, and boast, and that was exactly what my dad was to me. He was my dad, my role model, my hero, and most of all, my friend. He was in the Air Force so he was not at home much, but when he was we did everything together. I remember sometimes I would be sleeping when he came home and he would come into my room and put me in a headlock to wake me up. Every time he did so, I gave him a beat-down. Of course, our favorite past time was watching wrestling.

There I would be watching WWF in the arms of my father. I would see "Hulk Hogan" or the "Junk Yard Dog" do a move and I would decide to try it on my dad. Now my dad was about six feet tall and almost two hundred pounds while I was two and a half feet tall weighing a good thirty-five pounds, yet, there I was trying to throw him on the ground and put him into the camel clutch or the sleeper.

Needless to say, when that did not work I would go with a more basic move like the elbow, a leg drop or even a dropkick, but to no avail. He would wait until my energy was exhausted to pin me for the one, two, and three. Sometimes he would let me kick out and on rare occasions he even let me pin him. Oh what joy I would get from the simple act of him letting me win. Even though I knew he let me win, that built my self-confidence. First, I conquered my dad, and next the world.

My life's goal was to be just like my dad. I wanted to join the Air Force. I wanted to be a preacher. I wanted to wear nice clothes and drive fancy cars. I wanted to be the very essence of who my dad was. I wanted to be him so badly that I asked my mom could I change my name to be the same as his. *"Call me Junior"* was my motto.

My dad was also my guardian angel. No one could correct me or chastise me. The world was mine to conquer and anyone who told me otherwise would have to answer to him. Anything I wanted I got. And it was mine (not yours, but mine). No one had permission to touch me, or my things.

I did what I wanted despite whom I hurt. I remember him buying me a toy gun that used rubber BBs. Boy, did I have fun. I shot everyone, my cousins and my dog. I would play spy and try to sneak up behind people just to get close enough to shoot them. *"Direct hit,"* I would say, *"the enemy has been eliminated!"*

The only person I could not shoot was my sister. I was a mess and everybody knew it, but hey, you could not get to me unless you went through my dad. That was something no one wanted to do. Not my aunts, uncles, or grandparents. Not even my mom. Of course, this led to problems between the two of them.

A Father in the Eyes of His Son

But my playing spy was the least of their problems. The fact was, their marriage was falling apart. What the problem was, I did not know then. I know now just from observation and having more information. When I became old enough to ask, I did not because I did not want to know. Needless to say, my parents got a divorce while I was at the age of five.

Nothing could have prepared me for it. There were no signs of dissatisfaction. Furthermore, I only remember one time in which they were in a real bad argument. Maybe that was because I was outside playing most of the time. But one time I came in early and heard yelling. I went to the door to listen.

"Oh, dad is just laying down a few rules. He is supposed to. He is the man of the house," I thought. I did not think anything was wrong until I heard a different tone in my mother's voice. For the first time in my life, I heard my mother cry. That once tender and passionate voice now carried emotions of hurt and despair. At this point, life became serious to me (about as serious as it could get for a five-year-old child). Fun and games no longer mattered. My mom was crying.

I burst through the door and stopped, looking at both of them. Together, they were the foundation of my world and it seemed as if my foundation was crumbling. There I was staring at them with eyes of both love and hatred. As I began to cry, it felt as if hot tears were rolling down my face. There was silence in the room. No one, most of all me, had anything to say.

"Come on, Terry, let's go to the store to get some ice cream," my father said. "My son and I are going to the store. We'll be back."

That was typical of my father. Going to get some ice cream and a toy could solve any problem I had in the world. Money was his defense. Since he felt that way, so did I. As we were in the store, I asked him, "*What are you going to get mama?*" My five-year-old rationale was that material things could fix their problems just as it had brought peace to my soul and satisfaction to my stomach. Boy was I wrong. We both were.

Soon my father was off again. The Air Force called and he had to go. Of course, that was his job, so when he left I thought it was no big deal. I did not understand the day he left was the last day he would be the man of the house. As usual, before he drove off, he would hug my sister and me. This time before he left he told me, "*Son, daddy loves you. And he wants you to know that he'll always be there for you.*"

Innocently enough I said, "*I know.*" One last hug and he was gone.

I Wanted My Life Back

I had not realized it then, but my dad was no longer a constant part of my life. I know a lot of people claim that fathers can still be a part of their children's lives but there are many limitations. Maybe growing up without a father has skewed my perception, but a father is not someone who fits days, months, and years of quality time into his new schedule. To me, there is no such thing as moving on to a new life.

There is no substitution for having your very own father in your life and living under your same roof. The differences are similar to having your own car versus having to catch a bus. When you have your own car you can get up and go whenever you feel like it. It is a convenience that is greatly appreciated.

However, when you have to take the bus everywhere your livelihood depends on someone else. You have to worry about the schedule of the bus. You have to get to the bus stop early just so that you will not miss it, but then you have no guarantee the bus will not be late. And do not let the schedule change without you knowing: you could be waiting for hours, which is a waste of time.

Having a father provides the same type of convenience. Just having someone to run to when you scrape your knee or have a bad dream: having the ability to run into the arms of a protector who will calmly let you know that there is nothing to worry about. Having someone to give you your first level of love and acceptance despite what others think of you. Without a father a child will not have that.

You see my father was my life, and when he left he took my liveliness with him. Regardless of what experts say, I will never change my mind about the matter. I guess it is their research versus my experience. One responsibility of a father is to bring stability and security to his household. He cannot do that if he is not there (1 Timothy 5:8).

The biggest issue with most men is that they have dreams, big dreams, and when they do not seem to be able to achieve them, they tend to let go of those things and persons they feel are holding them down. That includes their wife and children. Their leaving makes the statement that they love their dreams more than they loved their family. And that is something most children, including myself, will never accept.

Do not get me wrong, as children, we can and will move on but our viewpoint is still the same. We dream of a life in which we would learn from our fathers and one day, for most boys, we long to be like him. However, when a father makes his dreams a priority over his children, we do not have the opportunity to glean from him.

This is true whether the father is in the household or not. If a father who is in the home does not make his children his top priority then they will have to deal with many of the things that a child without his father also deals with. If the truth be told, most of the time, men end up spending their time chasing the wind than actually catching their dreams. At the end of the day, most do not have anything to show for their actions.

What my father did not understand was he created a world for me in which I was the ruler. I answered to no one, for he was there to shield me. When he left, my fortress was made vulnerable. I still did as I wanted to, but now I had to answer for my actions, and everyone wanted to give me what they felt I deserved, especially my grandfather.

Before my father left, my grandfather could only desire to beat me. He used to tell me things such as *"I got a pile of switches waiting just for you and one day . . ."* That was my grandfather. He would never finish a threatening sentence. He would say things like, *"Boy, if I ever get hold of you . . .",* or *"If I ever catch you, why then . . ."* He would always try to get you to fantasize about the worst case scenario.

However, because my father was my shield, my response was always, *"You ain't gonna touch me 'cause if you do, why then . . ."* That was my way of letting him think of the worst case scenario. My grandfather was only five feet three inches tall and I just knew my father could body slam him.

My dad was my heavyweight champion of the world. But all that changed after he left. I remember one day I was outside playing with my cousins and my granddad came out to gain control of what was going on. I always played rough and I played to hurt. So, here comes grandpa with the same old line, *"Boy, don't make me catcha hold to ya'. I'll . . ."*

With all boldness and confidence, I said, *"You ain't gonna touch me."* And for some reason, I gave him more than just the regular spiel. This time I dared him.

"If you're so bad, take off your belt and beat me. I dare you. Go 'head if you're bad. My dad will beat you so bad . . ."

I went on and on. I was bold and my attitude was exceedingly arrogant. However, this time I noticed that my grandfather had taken off his belt. *He's just pretending*, I thought. Then he began to move in my direction. Still talking trash, I thought, *this man must be crazy trying to come up on me like this. Doesn't he realize that my father will beat him severely?*

I kept talking, but with every step my grandfather took, the confidence in my voice weakened. Soon I had stopped talking because I could not believe this man was about to beat me. With his belt in his hand, my grandfather raised his arm up to the heavens as if to acquire a special anointing of strength from God to beat me and with one swing, it began: my first beating.

A Father in the Eyes of His Son

This beating was a combination of all the beatings I should have received for everything I ever did. The beating was such a shock to me that I lost my breath and I could not breathe. It was like I experienced an electric shock, lightning, or something. Time seemed suspended. The only thing I remember was falling to the ground, gasping for air. Time resumed and in a little while, the beating stopped.

There I was on the ground gulping for air. By the time I could breathe again, the crying started. With my first breath of air, I let out a loud wail. The pain echoed throughout my flesh. I cried so much that even after I ran out of tears, I was still crying. The tears from my eyes cried because of the pain. The tears from my heart cried for revenge. They cried for my father to come home. The only thing I could think about was telling my father. Oh, I had dreams of my father and myself just beating my grandfather down. My dad was going to be my tag team partner. In the case of my grandfather, there would be no tag but a constant double team. Forget the rules. Call for disqualification. I did not want to win this match. I wanted revenge. So I waited.

The tip of my tongue longed for my dad's arrival while my eyes burned with hatred toward my grandfather. Every time he saw me he said, *"I told you I was gonna get you one day. Keep on, and I'll get you again."* The whole time, I would just stare at him with the threatening eyes of a five year old.

If I could I would have taken on my grandfather by myself, but I was no fool. Comparing me to my grandfather was like putting an unknown wrestler in the ring with a heavyweight, like "King Kong Bundy." The wrestler, Bundy, was a big boy, six feet nine inches and over four hundred pounds. All he had to do was give his opponent one stomach splash and the match was over. So I waited, patiently, knowing that one day my problem would be rectified.

However, my grandfather was the least of my problems. It seemed that every one, except me, knew my dad was not coming back. Soon everyone began taking (what I call) cheap shots at me. All of a sudden, I was no longer an untouchable. Even my cousins saw this as an opportunity to get back at me.

I remember us playing football, and, as usual, I played rough. This time I knocked my baby cousin down. I was about seven and he was two. Yeah, my motto was, *"You knew I played rough before the game started."* He started crying and his brother and sisters saw this as their chance to get me back for all the times I shot them with my gun. In all, there were five of them.

"Hey, watch what you're doing. You can hurt someone," one of them said.

"Yeah, don't you hit my little brother like that again or I'll hit you," said another one.

"Well, why don't you tell him to stay out of my way or I'll knock both of you down," I said as cocky as ever. I continued with, "Now what are you gonna do?"

Needless to say, not only did one take me up on my bluff, but all five decided to take advantage of this. They were more than a family: they were a clan. If you fought one, you fought them all. There I was in the midst of a one-on-five Royal Rumble.

Before I knew it, the same beat down I wanted my dad and I to give my grandfather was being delivered to me. No rules. No disqualification. And worst of all, there was no one for me to tag. My partner had left the ring post and was nowhere to be found; and as more of these instances occurred, the more and more I felt deserted and abandoned. It was like I was in this fight *alone*.

The "Big" Little Man of the House

One day while I was at the dinner table with my mother and sister, I was already beginning to figure out that my dad was not coming back when my mom told me words I would never forget. She said, *"Terry, you should know by now that* your father isn't coming home. You now have to take on the role of being the man of the house." Man of the house? I had just started school and was learning my ABCs and now I was the man of the house! The very essence of those words seemed to eat away at my childhood. I could even feel the household burden being transferred to my shoulders.

A sense of responsibility entered my life and I felt as though I was now to be the protector, the comforter, and the stronghold for the family. I was the only man in the house; therefore, I had to do the man's job because a woman could not do it, so I thought. Thus, I had to take on a lot of responsibility around the house.

One of my mother's goals in raising me was that a man must assume responsibility for his family. She was often quoted as saying, *"I'm not going to have a sorry man as a son."* Little did she know that those were my sentiments exactly. When I found out my parents were divorced, I made a promise to myself at the age of five, *"Things won't be this way when I get married. When I find my wife, I'm gonna give her the world."*

From that point on, I became real focused on knowing what it would take to become a good husband and father. I was literally the man of that house. I remember one time some boy stepped up to my sister trying to play his game. I was around seven years old but I stepped up to him and said, *"Excuse me, do you have a job? What's your name? Where do you live? What can you do for my sister?"*

My sister yelled, *"Mom, tell him to stop! This ain't none of his business anyway."* Of course, she was mad because she liked the attention he was giving her. But what can I say, he could not do anything for her. Besides, I was the man of the house. Anyone who tried to talk to my sister had to come through me. It is still like that today. Anytime my sister starts to talk to anyone, before it gets serious, she comes and talks to me. Why? Because I am the man of the house. *(By the way, that boy left my sister alone).*

A Void

My whole world was falling apart and I was trying so desperately to hold it together by myself. But I could not. In the short time I'd been alive, the only persons I really knew were my mom and dad, and now half of my world was gone. There were other people around me all the time but I was never close to anyone except my father and mother. Now, I felt like a stranger amongst family. The void was so strong it silenced my soul and sent me into seclusion.

I became an introvert, not saying much, yet thinking deep thoughts in the midst of this dark situation. I became a thinker and spent much of my time doing so. As the saying goes, *still waters run deep*. I was always contemplating something. Sometimes these thoughts were the only thing that would brighten up my day. I pondered everything, but mostly I asked the question, *"Why?"*

Divorce affects every child in different ways, even though they may not say so. You must understand that a parent's leaving will affect their children much more than they will ever say. This is because the children do not know how to adequately express how they may feel. Most adults do not know how to adequately express how they may feel. Like many other children, I went into a deep depression because my protector and strong tower was no more.

When two people get divorced, there is no way they can be thinking about what is best for the children. They give the excuse that, *"I know that it is not best for the children, but this is what is best for me."* I do not care what the experts say, that is *selfish*.

Any marriage can work if each person is willing to lay down their pride through humility. However, we live in a world that is more focused on *self* than on others. When we observe our pride over the feelings of others, no mercy is given or received. And in divorce, the ones who get hurt the most are the children (Jonah 2:8).

There are people today who simply lose their mind because of some traumatic experience, yet, when people get divorced they accept the notion that *the children will be okay.* They fail to deeply consider the ramifications of their actions and they do not give it a second thought because the children do not verbalize how they feel. However, that is only because they do not know how to verbalize their pain.

I remember playing with my cousin's baby boy, but he was real quiet and not in his usual playful mood. I tried tickling him, but it did not work. So I pulled out all the stops trying to make him laugh, but all he did was stare at me (*maybe I just wasn't funny*). As I continued to look at him, I could see a spirit of heaviness round about him.

I asked him, "Is there something wrong?"

He nodded, *yes.*

"Do you want to talk about it?"

He shook his head, *no.*

"Do you know what it is?"

He hunched his shoulders, *I don't know.*

He was two years old and had a spirit of heaviness. When you are two years old, you should not have a long face because you have not experienced any long days. You should not be thinking about anything deeper than cartoons (and they have some deep ones today: I remember growing up on Looney Tunes). All I could do was wrap my arms around him and let him know that I loved him. But, the issue was he did not need to hear and feel that from me, he needed to hear that from his father.

You may be asking the question, *"How could you tell that there was a spirit of heaviness on him?"* I could tell because I noticed that it was the same spirit that I had to fight. Because of what I have been through, my spirit can easily pick up on the spirit of a child that is hurting. I know what it feels like to hurt and there is no one to talk to about it. When pain cannot be verbalized, it is kept within the heart and stays there like a bomb waiting to explode.

My grandfather told me a parable about playing around dry wood chips that have been sitting in the sun for days. On the outside, everything appears to be fine, but deep at the core, there may be an internal fire that has started due to the internalized heat. You do not see any flames and you do not smell any smoke so you assume everything is all right. Then one day you see this large pile of chips engulfed in flames because you did not take the time to periodically water the pile down. Likewise, parents need to constantly water their children with love.

For this reason alone, parents, especially single parents, need to learn how to communicate with their children. When a crisis like divorce happens, the children do not know who to talk to for a couple of reasons: 1. They may blame the parents for the divorce, or 2. They may blame themselves. In either scenario, the children have lost the bond of trust that had once been there. If a parents does not keep prying into the hearts of the children, the pain will never go away.

The Bond of Loyalty

My loyalty was pledged to my father because he is my father. I remember when my father would come home, sometimes I would be asleep and he would come wake me up by tickling me or simply letting me know that he was there. Other times, I would see him driving up into the drive way and I would run out of the house toward his direction. I could barely wait for him to get out of the car so I could jump into his arms and feel his security. Why did I feel secure in his arms? Because I was his child.

I remember my family going to the grocery store when I was young and I lost sight of my father. At the time my father had a small 'fro. I thought to myself, *if I see the afro I will find my dad*. I did not think about searching for my mother, I was in search of my father. I began to go throughout the store looking for my father's 'fro (it was the most distinguishable feature about him). Finally, I found the 'fro. He was a good distance away, so I quickly followed him. He was leaving the store, *and without me,* so I began to run after him. I got out of the store, turned the corner and yelled, *"Daddy, wait!"* He turned around only for me to find out it was not my father (but the afro was the same). I began to cry because I felt lost without him. Who would protect me? Who would play with me? Who would I emulate?

Shortly after I began to cry, I felt this reassuring voice in the background say, *"Here I am. Everything is going to be all right. Come here to daddy."* Before he could finish talking, I turned and ran into his arms. I was found. I was secure. I was in the arms of my savior.

When he left, my loyalty to him was shattered. I felt abandoned and left behind. I felt lost. Who would guide me through life? Did he not love me any more? What could possibly be more important than me? In my mind, nothing should have been. He placed following his dreams above helping me achieve mine.

In marrying my mother, he made a vow to love her forever. That vow included raising my sister and me. He that swears and keeps his word, even if it means he may lose out, will be a man honored by God, (Psalms 15:4). (*Even if that means letting go of the pursuit of your dreams just so you can be there for your child*). His loyalty was supposed to be pledged to me, but it was not. The consequence of that was I learned at an early age you do not give someone your loyalty *just because.*

Loyalty is given in reciprocation for the loyalty received from the one who is seeking it. In other words, if I want someone to be loyal to me, I must first prove that I will be loyal to him or her. Even God knows that we love Him because He first loved us (1 John 4:19). There must be some degree of trust established. Parents who have not gained the trust of their children will never receive their loyalty. The title of parent can never be taken away from you but the children's trust and loyalty towards you can. Furthermore, we, as children, go in search of people who will be loyal to us.

Everyone is born to a father and a mother. That father and mother is given the task and responsibility by God to care for that child and to teach that child. Every father and mother will be held accountable by God for how they raised their child. It does not matter under what circumstances the child is born, the child must be parented.

However, just like God gives us parents, the Devil will also try to provide for us parental figures that will try to influence us to go down the wrong path. When our parents neglect to do the smallest parental duty, the Devil comes in and does his best to fulfill that task with glamour, fortune, fame and fun.

When children have a strong relationship with their father the temptation to do something wrong will be countered by the thought of possibly losing the current relationship with their father. For some children, just knowing that they have let their father down causes them to cry. Why? Because that bond of loyalty is there and their father has made sure that all voids in their life are fulfilled.

Searching for Fulfillment

Proverbs 27:7 states: *"The full soul loatheth an honeycomb; but to the hungry soul every bitter thing is sweet."*

In this verse the full soul represents someone who feels complete. Children who do not feel voids in their lives are less susceptible to things that are a detriment to them. Since they feel full, they do not feel the need to go searching for something to fill the void in their lives. The only things that attract their attention are those things that are sweet to life. Why? Because they do not feel they have to settle for a snack, which gives temporary fulfillment, when their parents can provide a full course meal.

On the other hand, the latter part of that verse tells us the one who is hungry will settle for anything, even if it is bitter.

Something bitter represents those things that are not good for us; however, because of the temporary satisfaction it gives we believe it to be sweet.

Children, search for snacks: agents of temporary fulfillment. Different kinds of snacks that they find are gangs, drugs, alcohol, cigarettes, and premarital sex. These elements, and others, give them temporary fixes but not a permanent fulfillment. I did not experience all of the above elements but the ones I did were because I was trying to find something to heal my hurt and make my life whole.

No matter what I did, it did not suffice. Unlike many others, I did not try too much because I did find fulfillment.

Poem Based on Psalm 68: 5

A Father to the fatherless am I to he
Who only believes in me.
I'll be the Father you never had
To the point that you can even call me Dad,
Allow me to care for you
Through and through,
I'll even supply your every need
And cause your very works to succeed.
I sent my Son to give you new life,
Filled with peace, no bitterness or strife,
And when you come to me,
I'll take pleasure in you,
I'll love you just like
A real dad is supposed to.
A Father to the fatherless am I to he
Who only believes in me.

Chapter 2

A Son in the Eyes of the Father

The Creator of All Worlds

I remember being five years old and praying in my closet. To be honest, I always saw my grandmother and mother praying and I was just mimicking them. I really did not know if anyone was going to hear me. All I knew was my grandmother said that *God answers prayer*. So with the inquiring mind of a five-year old, I began to ask questions.

The questions I asked were as deep and developed as a five-year old could ask. The questions were sincere and from the heart. I told God that I wanted some toys and clothes. I mean He was God, right? The more I talked the deeper and more intimate the questions became. I began to prove God with hard questions like, *"why are there mean people,"* and *"why doesn't everyone love each other?"* Finally, I asked, *"When is my daddy coming home?"*

For the first time in my monologue to God, I paused as if I were waiting for a response. Silence, not even the air would whisper. All Heaven and hell stood quiet as if we were all waiting to see what God would say. Out of all the questions I asked, this one my five-year old heart wanted to know more than the others. As I quieted my soul in preparation of hearing, I heard a voice whisper into both my ears saying, *"I am a Father to the fatherless, and I'll be your father if you let me. Your every dream I'll bring true if only you'll allow me to."*

Can you imagine that? To actually hear the voice of God to many is beyond belief. However, it is that very experience that has kept me and helped me to become the person I am today. As Paul wrote to the church at Corinth, *"But by the grace of God I am what I am . . ."* (I Corinthians 15:10).

At that age, I did not have a good knowledge of the Scriptures, so I just believed what I heard was from God by faith. Today, I understand that God will not speak anything against His Word; therefore, anything that He ever told me would have to be based upon His Word. Much to my delight, I had a promise that God would be my Father and teach me how to be the man that He desires me to be (Psalms 68.5).

I believe there are two main reasons why I believed God would be my Father. The first was my upbringing by my mother and my grandmother. They continually offered up my name in prayer before the Lord God, especially my grandmother. My grandmother was an evangelist and a missionary. Every one in the town knew her and my grandfather as people of prayer.

Often times, they would go out to evangelize and knock on people's doors to tell them about Christ and pray healing prayers for the sick. On Saturdays, my grandmother would call all her children and grandchildren over to her house for prayer. We would start off with a song and then pray. During prayer, my grandfather would take anointing oil and anoint each one of the children and grandchildren.

As he would anoint us, my grandmother would call out our names before the Lord in prayer. This was done as a symbol that they were consecrating and dedicating us to the Lord.

After that, my grandmother would ask for one of us to get her the Bible, which was (and is) the first and final authority in all matters. Most of the time, she would read a text or passage herself. Other times, she would appoint one of us to do so. After which, she would give us a summary and always let us know (no matter what that text was; even if it was John 11:35, ("*Jesus wept.*") that Jesus was the soon coming King.

As kids, we really did not know what was going on; we just knew we had to come. My grandmother was a firm believer that *a family that prays together stays together*. Often times my grandmother would sit her grandchildren down individually and talk to us about Jesus Christ. She would sit me down and begin to talk about the love of Christ and you could feel that love in her every word. She was passionate about Jesus Christ. Much of that passion she had was instilled in my heart: that is why I believe the Word of God the way I do, and also why I believed that God would be my Father. I was taught to believe the Word of God.

But the main reason why I believed God would be my Father was because my heart was so desperate for a father I would have accepted anything to fill that void. Like I mentioned in the previous chapter, children will search to fill any void in their lives. As a parent, you need to understand what voids your child may have so that you can have a say in how that void is filled.

For example, if people), whether child or adult, are void of attention, they will begin to act in a way that will cause them to receive it, either positive or negative. The following examples show how a person will call for negative attention. I remember seeing a guy try to give a pick up line to a girl, but she was not paying him any attention until he called her a derogatory name. After he said that, he had more than enough attention from her. She even gave him a reply much along the same lines of the statement that he gave her.

Another example is that of a child who does not get the love and attention they need at home and, as a result, they join gangs. Why? There is a need for love and feeling bonded to a family, and since they feel they get that from the neighborhood gang, they join it. If a son knows that when he gets home his father is going to be there for him and will even take time to share with him in recreational activities, help with homework, or even just to talk, that son is less likely to entertain doing such things.

On the other hand, children can also have a void of trust. This is the case when the parent seemingly is overbearing and places that child in a box. That child develops a sense of a void (I say a sense of a void because the world has nothing to offer). When that child begins to leave home he or she will begin to experience other things with other children. They will begin to yearn for more breathing room. As stated before, a parent needs to know and understand the voids in their child's life so they can have that void filled, yet in the proper way. My void was filled by Jesus Christ at an early age; therefore, I did not get into a lot of things, though I did stray on many occasions.

Another reason why I did not get into a lot was because I became a person of solitude.

I was a thinker: introspective if you will. However, I was not truly alone. God was and always is right there with me (Hebrews 13:5).

I would often times seem to talk to myself (because no one can see God in the natural). I would ask Him questions and He would answer me. Furthermore, He taught me I could not fill an internal void with external things. I would get toys but they would get old. I would have friends but they would get on my nerves. But God living on the inside of me, that brings me new mercies every morning (Lamentations 3:23).

An Everlasting Love

Because God promised to be my Father, I demanded a list of things from Him just like I had done from my natural father did. My rationale was that my natural father gave me what I wanted and if God was going to take his place, He would have to do the same. And He did because He promised He would.

Just like natural fathers want to bless their children so will our heavenly Father bless us out of His love for us (Luke 11:9-13).

Can you believe that? God was willing to prove to me He loved me. He gave me a promise that whatever I needed He would provide. And that is exactly what He did. God honors me because I honor Him. Some of my decorative awards/positions included being the State President for the South Carolina NAACP Youth and College Division. During my tenure, I won the National Medgar Evers Leadership Award in 1998. Other positions I held included being on the West Columbia Youth Leadership Institute Steering Committee in 1998 as well as the Collaborative for Community Trust.

I was nominated Brother of the Year by my fraternity, Alpha Phi Alpha Frat., Inc., for the 1997-98 school year at the chapter, state and regional level. I made it to the National Competition because of these accomplishments, however, I was disqualified because I came to the interview late. That was my fault and I could not blame God for my mistake. I overslept.

I was also identified by The State Newspaper, in South Carolina, as one of the Top 10 Minority Role Models in the State of South Carolina. The article was headlined, *10 to Watch*, in a special that was done during Black History Month in 1998. These are only a few of the awards and honors for which I received recognition. God made me a role model to the community. That is exactly what He said He would do in His Word. He made me a light to others, according to Matthew 5:14. That is what a role model is, one who provides a light for others to follow. And what did I do when I received honor? I let people know that it was because of God in my life that I am who I am (1 John 4:18). Because God is a God of honor, He makes His children people of honor.

I remember how I got the job at Ford Motor Company. I went to a career fair in Atlanta, Georgia. The night before, I prayed to God saying, *"Father, I really want to work at Ford Motor Company. You said that I could ask you anything in Jesus' name and I could have it. I know that your Word is good and I thank you for it, in Jesus' name, Amen."* The next day, I went to the career fair and passed out several resumes, but I had a special resume I prayed over the night before and I was going to give that resume to the Ford representatives.

Well, I gave it to them and nothing happened. They told me they would look over my resume and if it looked like I could match a position they had open, they would give me a call. About two months later, I received a call from someone at Ford Motor Company. Within a year's time, I had an interview. Four months after that, I had a position (and this is the abridged version of this blessing).

Why was God so good to me? Because He is my Father. Even more importantly, I was obedient to Him by keeping by keeping His statutes and commandments. Many people have accepted Jesus as Lord of their life, but they have not officially made God their Father. You do this by obeying His Word. When you do this, you too will begin to see the glory of God impact your life. It will not be an overnight thing; it will be an *overtime* thing. If you will stay with God through it all and exercise patience, He will do the same for you that He did for me (Galatians 6:9).

I want you to also know that not only was God good to me when I was being obedient, but He was good to me even when I missed some things. I may fall, as I have in times past, but even then I have a promise that God will not forsake me; instead, He will uphold me with His right hand (Psalm 37:24). God is like a natural father who takes responsibility for his children.

In some cases, I was like a prodigal son who went away on his own and had to experience trials (things I went through because I was away from God's protective covering) in order to realize that I needed God. God's response to me when I finally came to my senses was the same as the father of the prodigal son (Luke 15:11-31). The attitude of his father upon his return was one of gratitude and love. He may not have approved of the things his son did while away but his only concern was that his son was finally home. With joy the father received his lost son home. When you make mistakes, God is right there to accept you back with no questions asked. Why? God is full of mercy, grace, compassion, and goodness. Not only will God accept you as His child, He will also treat you as if the mistake never happened.

In understanding ancient cultures and traditions, it was a disgrace for a son to leave his father before the time. In some cultures, if and when a prodigal son would return home, as he would walk the street returning to his father's house the people of the community would throw fruits and vegetables at him to express their disgrace for what he did.

The reason the father ran out to meet his prodigal son was to walk his son back home. The father walking his son back was a way of the father shielding his son from the shame the community would have shown by throwing things at him for his disgraceful act. This was the father's way of showing the community that his son was accepted home. Just like this natural father, our heavenly Father has the ability to cover our sins.

God Is Not Your Problem

When you come to realize how much God loves you and how good He truly is, you will not have a problem believing His goodness. The Lord definitely is good all the time. However, many people do not believe that God will do good things for them because of two main reasons:

(1) They fail to realize God working in their everyday life.

(2) They blame God for things that have gone wrong in their lives, which is the most widely recognized reason.

Both of these things, if overlooked, can cause you to doubt God's goodness, and even in extreme cases doubt God's existence.

The first thing you must realize is God is working everyday in your life. The small things that God does for us often time go unrecognized because of the trials and tribulations we face in our lives. You must begin to recognize the little things (at least they seem little), God does. For example, God allowed you to wake up this morning with your right mind, the ability to breathe, and so forth; yet, many fail to give God five seconds to tell Him five words, *"Thank You for life's breath."*

Not only that, but there have been times in your life when you have been shielded from trouble. God made a way of escape for you even though you knew you were in the wrong place at the wrong time doing the wrong thing. Nevertheless, God's mercy kept you from being consumed (Lamentations 3:22, 23). Some of you may have habitually said, *"Thank God I got out of that."*

You may say life is bad, but it could be worse. I want you to think about a time when a way was made out of no way. Think about a time when you could not see your way out, but you received a miracle just in time. Whether you knew it or not, it was because of God's mercy that the situation did not consume your life.

I know personally that there were many times in my life that if it had not been for God protecting me from my own ways and mistakes I would either be in jail or dead. But God's grace and mercy were there to keep and protect me, just as a father protects and covers his child when he makes a mistake. A child may do something foolish, but a good father will recognize, not what the child did, but why the child did it, and deal with the why. Once the "why" is dealt with then the "what" will no longer be an issue because the "why" is the root. If you kill the root the tree (or the what) cannot survive.

You may be saying, *"If God is God, why is the world such a bad place?"* Your rationale is saying, because the world is a bad place there must not be a God. You fail to realize that God is not the one causing you trouble. There are three groups from which trouble comes: (1) demons, (2) other people, and (3) ourselves.

The first one identified is demons. The Devil's job is to steal, kill, and destroy (John 10:10). Satan is the one who does not want you to live a good and prosperous life and he will do any and everything to make sure you do not. His job is to try his best to defeat you (note: he can only try). However, if you are not sober, doing things in a right mindset, vigilant, and alert to situations around you, the Devil will be able to devour you. (1 Peter 5:8).

The trick of the enemy is to attack you and then try to get you to question why God is not doing anything about your situation. That is what Satan did to Job. He told God if he was allowed to attack Job then he could get Job to curse Him. That is what the Devil does when he attacks you: he tries to get you to curse or doubt the Living God. In the end, Job had to receive a deeper revelation of God's love for him before his restoration was manifested (Job 42:5).

So many times we only know God based upon what we have heard in our Sunday school classes and Sunday Services. In many cases today, we seem to learn about God from people who doubt His very existence. There are many people of other beliefs who know more about the Bible than many Christians do. When they question us about what we believe, many Christians stumble because they do not have a firm foundation with God. A firm foundation comes from having a relationship with God and knowing Him.

It was not until Job realized God was not only God, but He was also a loving Father who cared for him, that his blessing came. Guess what: God cares for you too. But you say, *if God cares for me, why won't He do something about my situation?* Well, God has done something about your situation, but unless you have knowledge of it, it will do you no good.

If you do not understand God loves you, and that He only wants the best for you, and you have no knowledge of His Word, then Satan can take advantage of you. (2 Corinthians 2:11).

This is the main reason why many marriages are destroyed. Satan comes in and deceives a person into thinking, *if I get out of this marriage, things will be better.* That is a device of Satan. Let us not be ignorant.

The second group identified is other people. For example, I grew up without a father in the home. As a result, things were much harder for me than they should have been. However, God did not cause my father to leave. My father left in search of a better life. That was a decision he made. Therefore, a lot of the turmoil in my life was because my father was not there, not because of anything God did. God allows mankind to make their own decisions: He has given man freewill. God has promised man a good life, but man has to choose to accept it.

Man, by his own choice, chooses how he will treat you. If he treats you good it is because he chooses to. If a person robs you it is because they made a decision to, not because God hates you or wants you to suffer. God wants us, His children, to love one another as Christ loved us. God wants people to treat us right but that must be balanced with our treating others right as well.

That last statement leads us to the third reason identified as to why life is sometimes bad: because of ourselves. Have you ever done anything bad? Did you ever hear your conscience tell you not to? Did you do it anyway? Did anybody make you do it? Was there a severe consequence for doing it? The answers to the previous questions are most likely yes, yes, yes, no and yes, respectively. When we do things, we have to understand for every action there is going to be an equal or greater reaction.

You have to learn to take responsibility for your own actions, because whether you like it or not, you will be held accountable. Many men today have fathered children but they dodge paying child support. That is a decision they make based on the thought they won't be held accountable, therefore, they do not have to take the responsibility. That is one thing both

A Son in the Eyes of the Father

God and my mother instilled in me: take responsibility for what you do.

In the sixth chapter of the book of Judges, we learn about the story of Gideon being called by God to lead the nation of Israel out of their bondage. However, one of the things that Gideon has an issue with was the fact that they are in bondage to begin with. Like Gideon, when God is trying to deliver us from our current circumstances, we are often so focused on the circumstances that it becomes hard for us to clearly see and accept God's way out of the situation.

Furthermore, we are looking to, and waiting for God to do something when God is telling us to stand up and overcome the situation at hand. If fact, many times the issue arises because of something we caused. We must understand and accept that our actions have consequences. Israel was in bondage because of their doings but Gideon wanted to blame God for not being there to protect them, when the truth is, it was Israel who left God's protection.

Many of us are saying, *the Lord has forsaken us,* when the truth of the matter is we have forsaken God. Our blaming God takes the responsibility off the Devil, other people, and ourselves, while we mistakenly, and with much audacity hold God accountable for what He did not do.

Israel was delivered into the hands of the Midianites because they forsook God. Likewise, in many areas of our lives we forsake God; thereby, leaving ourselves open to the tricks of the Devil. Why is it important for us to know God is not responsible for our problems? Once we understand God is not trying to do us wrong, we will stop blaming Him for *our* problems. Furthermore, when we fully begin to comprehend His love for us, our problems will go away. Why? God will deliver us just as He did for the children of Israel, despite their disobedience.

Because I knew this, I did not blame God for something He did not do. I did not blame God for my father leaving. My father left on his own decision. Should God have stopped him? *No.* Did God want him to leave? *Definitely not!* However, God is not a tyrant who rules our lives and He was not about to force my father to stay with us. My father had a choice. We all do and God allows our choices good or bad. We must remember that with every decision there will be a consequence, good or bad. We have to accept Him into our lives, or He will not interfere in our lives. Furthermore, we have to accept His Word and allow ourselves to be lead by His Spirit (Romans 8:14).

Will you miss it? Yes. Will you be perfect? No. Will God forsake you? *Definitely not!* God did not say that He only loved those that were perfect or always on point. No, God said He loved the world, those who were dying in sin (John 3:16). God loves you *now.* He wants to form a relationship with you *now.* He wants to become your Father now! And God will teach you how to be His child.

Sonship

Even today, sometimes I ask God, *"Why do you love me so much?"*

His reply is simply, *"You are my son."*

Now, some people may be stuck over the fact that I believe I am a bona fide son of God, and because they do not believe I am a son of God, they will never believe, they too, can be a child of God. I am not saying that I am *the* Son of God (that is Jesus Christ); however, I have been given the Spirit of adoption (Romans 8:14,15).

Do you understand it? We have the opportunity to become beloved children of God. Why? In 1 John 4:19, it tells us *He first loved us.* That means that He loved us before we were ever born. He loves us even though He knew we would live lives of sin. We did not do anything to cause God to love us and we cannot do anything to cause God to hate us. But please understand, just because God loves us does not mean that He will not hold us responsible for our actions.

Because of His great love for us, God provided a way for us to become His children while we were yet sinners. When you understand this, you will also understand you cannot clean yourself up before you come to God. What God is saying is that if we come to Him, He will clean us up and make us new because that is His desire. God's desire is to recreate me so that I will be the man my family, community, business and this world needs. He wants to make me into a new man (2 Corinthians 5:17).

God wants to recreate who you are as well. How do I know? That is what He did for me and God is not a respecter of persons. However, like I said before, it will not happen overnight. My first experience with God was at the age of five. It was not until my latter years of college that I began to see God manifest himself on my behalf. It was over twenty years between the time when God first spoke to Abraham and when the blessing finally manifested. What am I saying? Allow God to take you through a process of change.

After we give our lives to God, we have to be renewed in our minds concerning His ways, wisdom, and character. Then we will be ready to inherit our blessings from God. However, as long as you are not taught the mature things of God, you cannot receive your inheritance. That is why you see many people today who are saved, but they are not seeing the blessings of God made manifest in their lives. They are still children from a spiritual standpoint. They are still going to Heaven, but they have not yet received the promise of abundant life after being born again.. (Luke 18:29, 30).

A Son Has Relationship

God gave the gift of salvation to the world, but not everyone will receive Jesus Christ as their Lord and Savior. God also made the gift of the Holy Spirit available to every believer, but not every believer will receive this gift of power. God has given each Spirit-filled believer power to overcome the world but many still live defeated lives because they do not know how to use this power. They have not been trained in the things of God.

Many Christians only have a religion of going to church and serving on the deacon board, the usher board, or singing in the church choir. Even some pastors only have religion. But in order to truly see the hand of God in your life, you must have relationship. You must have a constant relationship with God *as your Father,* and in order to do that you have to please Him. Even Jesus had to please God.

To be a true son of God you must please Him. Jesus, understanding this concept, said in Matthew 12:50 that anyone who considered themselves as either a brother or sister of His had to be doing the will of the Father. God is ready to prove himself to you as a Father but the real question is *"Are you willing to prove yourself as a son?"*

My Father and I

I in him and he in me,
Our connectivity will forever be.
Who he is shapes who I am as I travel the road of life
On my way to being a man,
Seems like déjà vu as I do things only to
Find out he did them too.
Why? Because I was with him when he did them;
Though unborn I was there.
I was there as he completed something worthy of praise,
I was there when he committed his first sin,
I was there when he stood alone and fought at the age of ten.
I was there when his mouth filled with laughter,
I was there when his heart cried tears of sorrow,
I was a part of everything he did even though my life did not start 'til many days after then tomorrow.
Oh yeah, I was there; and
Just as Levi paid tithes unto Melchisedec the same time Abraham did while yet in his loins, I was there.
I in him and he in me,
Our connectivity will forever be.

Chapter 3

Created in the Image of My Natural Father

Just Like Him

Genesis 5:3 states: *"And Adam lived an hundred and thirty years, **and begat a son in his own likeness, after his image;** and called his name Seth."*

Let us take another look at this verse but first let us define two words: likeness and image. The word likeness refers to character; intrinsic qualities that makes a person distinguishable. The word image refers to physical reflection; exterior qualities that makes a person distinguishable. So let us read this verse again [with emphasis added]:

And Adam lived an hundred and thirty years, and begat a son in his own likeness [character], *after his image* [physical reflection]; *and called his name Seth:*

When people see me they immediately note the resemblance between my father and me. Even people who have not seen my father in fifteen years see me and say, *"You look just like your dad. Your dad could not deny you if he wanted to."* If the truth be told, I do. When he was my age I looked just like him. My prayer is that when I get to be his age I look a little bit different

(I do not want the receding hairline and the extra weight–still praying about the hairline).

The hardest thing about growing up without a father was that every time I did something wrong I would hear people say, *"You're gonna be just like your dad."* That really ate me up on the inside and I resented people when they said it. At that time in my life I did not want to be associated with him in that way, but they did not care. If I was acting badly they would say, *"You're gonna be just like your dad."* If I was being rebellious they would say, *"You're gonna be just like your dad."* If I forgot to take out the trash they would say, *"You're gonna be just like your dad."* Well, maybe that last one was an exaggeration, but still, they could have been more sensitive.

Fear of Being Him

I remember my father coming to my college graduation. I met him, my sister, and my mother at a particular restaurant. They arrived before I did by a few minutes. Because I was running late, they decided to go ahead and order. Well, I arrived approximately five minutes afterward and sat down at the table. The waiter came over to take my order and I ordered my favorite dish at the time, which was the full slab of baby back ribs meal. As I completed my order, my mother and sister just looked at each other and laughed.

I looked at them like they were crazy. They knew good and well that my favorite dish at that time was the full slab of ribs, so I was wondering what was going on. For the next minute or so they would just look at me and giggle. I was thinking to myself, *Okay, are they laughing with me or at me? Or is it just an inside joke that I don't know about.*

Finally, I said, "What is so funny?"

My sister asked, "Why did you order the ribs?"

"Because that's my favorite dish." I said emphatically.

"Guess who else has that as their favorite dish?" My sister asked coyly.

"Who? Mom?" I asked.
She nods *no*.
"You?" I asked again.
She nods *no*.
"Who? Dad?" I asked for the last time.

She just laughed. I was thinking *big deal* until she said, *"You guys are just alike."*

When she said that, I just blew it off. Later that night, we went back to the hotel where he was staying to watch television and talk. He was lying on the couch and I was lying on the bed. We were both watching television minding our own business until, you guessed it, my sister comes around with a camera and takes a picture of us. "Come, look mom. They even have the same posture while lying down."

I looked at him. He looked at me. We both were lying back with our feet crossed, hands behind our head and focusing on nothing but the television. Chances are we were both thinking the same thing too: *Get out of the way; you're blocking the television.* Again, I blew it off.

Another time, I remember calling my mother just to talk and see how she was doing. When I addressed her on the phone I did so in a joking manner as if I was trying to flirt with her. She said, *"Bill, is that you?"* Bill? Who is Bill? I was thinking to myself, *my momma is talking to someone named Bill and did not let me know.*

I said, "Mom, this is your son. Who is Bill? Are you talking to somebody?"

"No," she said, "I thought you were your father. You sound just like him."

Okay, now I am beginning to think. I look like him and I sound like him. That should not be a big deal because I am his son. I have his DNA. However, I never knew that ribs were his favorite dish. Nor did I ever pattern myself after his posture. But these were the least of my worries.

I remember making a decision about something and my sister said, *"Dad would have done the same thing. You two even think alike."* Now I am beginning to analyze myself because I have always wanted to position myself to not think like him or I would make the same mistakes as he did. But the big clincher was when he came into my room and said, *"Yeah, I have the same exact comforter."*

Then I became fearful because I was seeing that even though he did not raise me, I had his character. My father left while I was five years old, yet I liked what he liked and hated what he hated. We even had similar goals and ambitions in life. He wanted to work for Cadillac as a mechanic: I wanted to work for Ford as a mechanical engineer. He wants to be a pastor: I feel I have a call on my life for ministry.

More and more I began to see my life was a replication of his. When he has a problem he deals with it internally by not addressing it with the people he has the issue with. When I have a problem in life I, for the most part, keep it to myself. My life was becoming a replication of his life, both mentally and physically. Mentally, I had his thought patterns and comprehended things the way he did. I even reacted to things the way he did. Physically, I have his external characteristics, even his voice. Growing up, I thought having my hairline recede was going to be the only characteristic of my father I would probably have to deal with. Now, that became the least of my worries. I made a vow that I would not be him, and there I was being exactly like him.

I felt like a failure. Everything I tried, all the hard work not to be anything like him, failed. I broke down and cried. I am going to be like my father, I thought. I am like him and he is like me. We are one and identical no matter what the distance between us may be. The more I thought on this matter the more hatred began to burn within. Was this my destiny? If so, how could I escape it? How could I go through life and not make the same mistakes he did if I did not even have to observe him to be like him?

The fact of the matter is, as young men, we often make the same mistakes that our fathers made because they never taught us. The reasons some fathers do not teach their children about their mistakes are: (1) The father is absent. (2) The fathers do not recognize their actions as a mistake. (3) The mistake happened in the fathers past and they don't want to expose current parts of their lives to their children. When it gets to us, the mistake becomes normal and rational because we do not know any better. It is a part of our nature. Without a father there to teach us how not to do things and how to do things, we go through life the best we can, many of us never getting it right.

The Child Must Learn From the Parent's Mistakes

That is what happened for Abraham and his son, Isaac. Abraham made a mistake and did not teach the lesson he learned to Isaac. Let us take a look at a mistake Abraham made before Isaac was born and Isaac making that same mistake later on in life. Why? He was never taught.

In Genesis 12:11–13, we see one of the flaws of a true man of God, Abraham. In this passage of history we see Abram (this was before God changed his name to Abraham) tells his wife, Sarai, (God had not yet changed her name either) that he wants her to tell people they are brother and sister because he was afraid for his life. Sarai was so beautiful that Abram felt that the men of Egypt would take his life in order to have her. However, Abram wanted to live even if that meant having to give her up. Luckily for Sarai, God intervened where Abram did not.

Now let us cut Abram some slack because God had not yet changed his name to Abraham, the father of many nations and the father of faith. I am sure when Abram became Abraham all that changed, right? Unfortunately not, in Genesis 20: 1, 2, we see Abraham doing the same thing.

Even when Sarah was almost ninety, she is described as being so beautiful that it causes Abraham to cower in the face of adversity again. Well, the same thing happens again. King Abimelech takes Sarah, now the mother of many nations, to be his wife. God, again, stepped in and brought upon the women of Abimelech's household the same curse that He was delivering Sarah from, and they all became barren. They stayed barren until Abraham prayed for them.

Now a short time before this occurrence, God told Abraham that Sarah was going to bear a child within a year's time (Genesis 18:10, 14). If God had not intervened this second time, Abraham would have never received Isaac as his son because Sarah would have borne Abimelech a child had he slept with her, and thereby, Abraham would not have received the blessing. However, God said through Sarah he would receive the blessing of a son (Genesis 17:19).

All of this happened before Isaac was born. As a result, Isaac never saw his father falter after this manner. However, later on, Isaac is confronted with the same scenario. Isaac responds the same way Abraham did. Rebekah, like Sarah, was very beautiful. Because of this, Isaac, responded in the very same way his father, Abraham, did. (Genesis 26:9). I guess the saying is true, *like father, like son.* Why would Isaac do this? It appears he never learned from his father's mistakes.

Isaac was not around when his father made the same mistake twice, so he never knew that his father responded the same way. When he was confronted with the same situation, he did the same thing. Why? As sons, we are not only patterned after our father in a physical manner, but a spiritual and mental manner also. A father must recognize his past failures and transfer that knowledge to his son so that his son will not make the same mistakes he did.

Here is another example of someone making a mistake because their father did it, but thought that it was the normal thing to do so he did not see it as a mistake. David, the greatest king of Israel aside from our Lord Jesus Christ, was great indeed; however, he did have some flaws. He loved women. As soon as David realize that God had established him as king of all Israel, one of the first things he did was marry more women (2 Samuel 5:13).

Like I said, David loved women. As king, he could have any woman he wanted. What woman would not want to be a queen? Furthermore, in those days, you did not tell a king no. That was unheard of. Queen Vashti did that to king Ahasuerus, king of one hundred twenty-seven provinces of Persia and Media. She may have told the king no, but she did regret it. Her royal estate was given to someone else, Esther. (See Esther 1.) This was the case with any king, and such was the case with David when he stole Bathsheba from his servant, Uriah. (See 2 Samuel 11.)

However, David's love for women not only affected him, it also affected Solomon, the son of Bathsheba, who grew up in a house full of women all espoused to his father. David did not teach Solomon by example, and therefore, Solomon followed in his father's footsteps because he thought his actions were normal and not sinful. In fact, history tells us that Solomon married over seven hundred women and had three hundred additional concubines or mistresses (1 Kings 11:1, 3).

Solomon did these things because David did these things. He learned this from his father. Because his father, David, did not have control over that part of his life, Solomon never thought anything was wrong because in his household it was normal. Part of a father's duty is to set an example for his children to learn from. This may mean the father needs to identify those areas in his life where he is faltering and do what is necessary to change.

A son has a passionate desire to be like his father, and thereby, patterns himself after the like manner. Whether right or wrong, the son will aim to be like his father. It is in our spirit to do so. That is why Jesus said He only did those things that pleased His Father (John 8:29).

We know that David was a great king. He was called by God as a man after God's own heart. David is the one who delivered the children of Israel from the Philistine giant, Goliath. David is the one who trained the most notable army for Israel and brought the nation its greatest feats. However, this was one area in David's life he needed to straighten out. As a result of David's sin, Solomon had to deal with this same area in his life. This fault caused Solomon's son to loose ten tribes out of the kingdom of Israel.

As a father, any area of your life you do not address, your children will confront. As children, we see our parents as the ones who we should emulate, whether they are good or bad. This is why so many times we see children fall prey to the same thing their parents did: they grew up thinking it was okay because their parents did it.

If you do not overcome that issue, trial, situation, or whatever, your child will have to battle with it. Dealing with areas of fault in your life is not only for your benefit but also for the benefit of your children. Leave a legacy of success for your children lest it be said about your child's failure, like father, like son.

One time as I was teaching this lesson to some young men in a juvenile detention center the reality of this principle really struck me when one of the young men raised his hand and said that the very first crime he committed was also the very first crime his father committed. The next thing I knew one hand after another began to raise as each young man began to identify areas of their life in which they were exactly like their fathers.

Men can no longer just do as they please and not think that their actions only affect them. No man is an island and we do not live in a box. Our actions today will affect our seed for generations to come. Based upon what we do today, our children will either live under a blessing or a curse. Even though Abraham and David had flaws, there relationship with God caused their seed to have favor based upon what their fathers did. In other cases, what a father does can bring destruction to his entire household.

The Effects of an Unloved and Untaught Child

Children are a gift from God but they are also a responsibility. Part of that responsibility is to teach our children life lessons so that they will not make the same mistakes. You cannot teach them if you are not there.

Let's look at an example that shows how the impact of a father not being there impacts the life of a son. Ishmael was fourteen years older than Isaac. After Isaac was weaned, Abraham threw a feast in his honor. I would have too if I had a child at age one hundred and Sarah was now ninety. Sarah saw Ishmael making a mockery of the whole situation and in turn told Abraham that she did not want Ishmael in the same house as their son, Isaac (Genesis 21:10-16).

Sarah did not want Ishmael, who was around the age of fifteen to sixteen, to have anything to do with Isaac nor Abraham, his father, anymore. The sad thing is that it was Sarah's idea for Abraham to sleep with Hagar, the Egyptian handmaid who bore Ishmael. Now she is throwing them out all together. Abraham did not want to do it, but he did because he knew that having the two in the same house was not going to work. Hagar and Ishmael were sent on their way with not even enough to survive.

Imagine being in the Middle East, which is mostly desert. You are sent to survive on your own and on your way out you are given some bread and a (the word "a" denotes one) bottle of water. How are you going to survive off of that? Would you say Ishmael was a bit bitter? Not only that, but on their way back to Egypt, Ishmael almost died. Only his mother was there to care for him. Trust me, I have been there; having to deal with bitterness because you experience something so traumatic and your father is not there to see you through is not easy to forgive (it is forgivable though).

A father is supposed to be someone you can go to in your time of weakness. He is a protector. In this case, Abraham was not there to help Ishmael. The Bible does not say, but I am sure that Ishmael was thinking in the back of his mind, I now have to be the "man of the house." When this task is placed upon the shoulders of a young man, it will lead to bitterness and unforgiveness. Unforgiveness leads to hatred, envying and strife (James 3:16).

Ishmael's unforgiveness was piled on top of the fact Sarai despised him ever since he was conceived (Genesis 16:1–6). At one point before he was born, his mother, Hagar, fled away from her mistress, Sarai, because of the hardship, which tells you that Ishmael was born into a tense situation. When a child is born into a tense situation where he or she is not receiving the necessary love needed but is constantly under ridicule, that child will usually become a rebellious person.

In Genesis 16:11, 12, God begins to tell Hagar about the child that she is going to have. The first thing that He tells her is that she will bear a son and that his name is to be called Ishmael, because He has heard her affliction. Many times we are in situations that we did not create but still the burden lies on us to bear it. We are afflicted and there is nothing that we can do about it.

Hagar could not refuse Abraham because he was her master. Hagar did not ask to be placed in the middle of the situation. She was placed into this circumstance because Sarah and Abraham stepped out of faith. Do to their unbelief, they created an Ishmael, meaning they created unwanted circumstances because of a wrong decision. And even though unfair, the burden for their actions were not carried by them, but by a now single parent mother named Hagar.

God went on to tell her a little about the character Ishmael would have. The first thing that He said was that Ishmael would be a wild man, or someone who is uncontrollable. In other words, he would be a person without regard for authority. Not only that, but his hand would be against every man and every man against his hand. This means that Ishmael would have the mentality that no one was for him and that every one was trying to take him down: he would trust no man.

Lastly, God said that he would dwell amongst his brethren. That word brethren was not referring to his half-brother, Isaac. It was referring to people of like minds. This is interesting because it helps us to understand that people who are born in similar circumstances as Ishmael desire to cling to others whom they can relate to.

In finding that group of people, they form their self-made family. People who join gangs have this mentality. What mentality is this? The Bastard Mentality. Interestingly enough, the Hebrew word for bastard, *mamzer*, means to be of mixed origins. Ishmael, of course, had a Jewish father (Abraham) and an Egyptian mother (Hagar). This made him a bastard by both the Hebrew traditional meaning of the word bastard and the context in which the word is used today.

Now God did not prophesy this to Hagar, because that was the way God created Ishmael. God prophesied this to her because He knew under the circumstances of the situation that kind of atmosphere would produce that kind of child. The atmosphere was not conducive to raising a child in the nurture and admonition needed. Ishmael was never given the proper love he needed to develop the right way.

I am not saying that he should have been heir along with Isaac; however, what I am saying is he never experienced the necessary atmosphere a child needs to be brought up in. If a child feels he or she is the source of confusion that can cause very adverse affects on the child. Because of Ishmael's experiences in his life and his hatred towards Isaac, the Arabs, even today, have a deep hatred towards the Jews.

The Bastard Mentality

When a father is not involved in the life of his son, the son loses out on learning from his father's successes and mistakes. Furthermore, when the son is tempted and tried, he will think himself through the situation the same way his father did because, even though the father is not there, they are connected in spirit.

Fathers, your life's goal should be to make sure your children have the tools to succeed even in areas where you have failed. Your heart should be towards your children, because you had better believe their hearts are fixed on you. Each generation should be going from glory to glory always attaining unto the measure of Christ. When this is not the case, we find ourselves living under what is known as a generational curse (Numbers 14:18). Fathers must understand their children will have to deal with the sins they leave unresolved. In 1 Kings 13:34, we see judgment for sin was passed upon a man named Jeroboam. Please note this thing became sin *unto the house* of Jeroboam, not just Jeroboam. Just to give you some context of this situation, Jeroboam was made king of ten of the twelve tribes of Israel. Even though God made his house great in the land, he turned and served other gods; he also caused the nation to serve other gods. Because of this, his action became a sin unto his entire household.

Jeroboam was responsible for dealing with the sin in his house and he did not do it. In fact, he was the one who introduced sin into his house. Furthermore, because he was king, he caused the nation of Israel to follow in his footsteps. In reading the next chapter, we see that Jeroboam's son, Abijah died, and in chapter fifteen, we see that his whole household died (1 Kings 15:29).

As a father, you must over come the trials you face so the curse will not continue on to your children. The areas of life you conquer will be the pedestal your children start out on.

On the other side of that, the areas of life you fail in will be the ditch that your child will have to climb his or her way out of.

According to Numbers 13:18, not only will the immediate children have to deal with the iniquity, but even the grandchildren and the great grandchildren will have to deal with the consequences. Someone has to take the responsibility and say, *"I am going to stop the curse in my family. It ends with me."* As a father, when you overcome an issue you are also empowering your future descendants to be able to do the same. That is where your heart should be.

Malachi 4:6 states: *"And he shall turn the heart of the fathers to the children, and the heart of the children to their fathers, lest I come and smite the earth with a curse."*

If the heart of the father is not with the child, then society as a whole is impacted. If you will look at the communities with the most crime, the most violence, the most gang activity and the most health issues, you will find that these communities lack one common element: fathers. Fathers missing in the community is also a high source for poverty, which leads to other issues. These communities lose their identities every time they lose a father.

Furthermore, it results in children being called *bastards*. The child did not do anything to deserve this. It was the father shunning responsibility that brought this upon the child. The word bastard denotes an illegitimate child, or someone who is fatherless. However, to use modern day vernacular, the word *bastard* also denotes someone who is characterized as being unruly, rebellious, and disrespectful to authority. The underlying connotation is the thought: *Didn't their father teach them how to behave?* A child, whether the father is there or not, who is deemed as such is thought of as not having a father to train them in the proper manner. In most cases, this is true. There are some cases where the child is just disobedient; however, the former occurs in greater proportions. We see these kids all the time and we become critical of them. How do I know?

I grew up without a father, and because that was the case, I had a real hard time submitting to male authority. I would do my job and be faithful at doing so; however, I looked at every man as being my equal. My thought pattern was, *you are not my father and even if you were, you were not there for me the times I needed you to be, so I do not owe you anything, especially my loyalty.*

As a young man, my thought pattern was: I am loyal to those who are loyal to me. Loyalty is earned; not given just because of who you are. I needed to know a person had my best interest at heart. Why? Because that trust had been broken in the past and I had a protective wall up so it would never happen again. I did not realize it then, but I had a bastard mentality. I was not going to take anything from anyone.

Part of my issue was that of survival. I had survived life for so long on my own that I saw myself as being equal to any man, young or old. I commanded respect. My bastard mentality was not as extreme as others, but still the mentality is the same no matter what level or degree of it you exhibit. Revisiting the situation surrounding Ishmael, he was never trained up in the way he should have gone.

Isaac, on the other hand, stayed in his father's house well into his manhood years. Isaac learned from his father, and when his father died, he received all his father had (Genesis 25:5). Ishmael, however, had to learn to survive for himself and take care of his mother. He learned to survive by any means necessary. Some of the things he learned to survive were good and some were not, but as the Scripture says in Proverbs 27:7b, "*. . . to the hungry soul every bitter thing is sweet.*"

This is the same mentality of many of my brothers (white, black, whatever color, it is just a shell) experience. It is a game of survival, and conflict arises when anyone seems to step in their way of doing it. Whether run-ins with their teachers, the law, or other family members, all they want is a little *respect*. In their mind, they are doing the best they can. Even though their thinking may be twisted, all they see is survival.

When they feel people are not respecting them, they will force respect at any cost. This results in fights, theft or robbery, and even murder. What you must understand is that these feelings all stem from the hurt and pain of not having a good father figure. And because a male figure has never chastised them, they will not accept it from any one else. We need that in our lives; but not just any male figure, we need it from the one in whose image we were created. We need our fathers.

The Broken Vessel – Psalm 51

In a room filled with Glory,
There stood a broken vessel,
Being extremely out of place,
How could any Glory be found in this vase,

Yet there it was placed,
By the Master on a table adorned with lace,
It neighbored vessels of gold and silver,
Each uniquely designed in its own way,
All glistening, and glaring in the light,
Making this broken vessel
Become an even more atrocious sight,

Some filled with diverse spices,
Of frankincense and myrrh,
But who would pour into this broken vessel,
Much less touch it lest being cut by a burr,
Yet, when the Master came looking for a vase to use,
This broken worthless vessel would be
the one He'd choose.

Yet, that vessel, though it was broken,
Would He cleanse and purge, then make a new mold.

The Refiner's Fire

In a whirlwind of fire was I spun round about,
Being purged but not consumed,
Tumbling about in a flame of molt,
The solidity of my life seemed to liquefy,
The height of my stature melting away,
My very existence beginning to flow.

There I am in a state of instability,
Only kept together by the crucible
in which I am contained,
My substance boiling into bubbles of vapor,
Yet I find myself still 100% me,
It's a feeling of being purified of outside influences,
And there I flow within the crucible.

In becoming my purest form am I poured out,
My liquidity conforms to the mold
in which I am entered,
I take the form of another yet I am still me,
And in the mold I stay until I solidify,
The boiling of my members congeal,
I become bonded together
And a vessel of gold I am now to be.

Chapter 4

Re-Created in the Image of My Heavenly Father

Seeing Myself Through Him

One thing I had to learn in life was that I had to view myself by the standards of God's Word. I could not allow myself to listen to what people said about me. People will judge you on your past and where you come from, which is really irrelevant. *For it matters not where you've been nor what you've done; however, it is where you are going today that will determine your outcome in life.* Furthermore, as a born-again believer, the old man (who I was) is passed away and the new man (who I am) is being developed (2 Corinthians 5:17) on a daily basis.

Also, we should not look at people based upon what they have done in the flesh (v.16). The word "flesh" is referring to life before knowing Christ as our Lord and Savior. When a person gets saved, he should no longer be held to the things of his past. He is, according to verse 17, a new creature. To be more concise, they are a re-created person in their spirit. Their body looks the same, but the change occurs on the inside.

Furthermore, this change on the inside shows up on the outside only after a process of time. Even though you are changed immediately on the inside, there are some things still in you that have to be dealt with. There are some things about you that have to change. You are being re-created into the image of God's Son, Jesus Christ (Romans 8:29).

No Longer a Bastard

Survival on my own was no easy thing. However, I managed to not only survive but to excel in life. When people would meet me and see me in action, their thinking was that I came from a wholesome background. (I did not in the sense my father was not there, but I did because God made up what was lacking).

When people would learn of the fact that I did not have a father in the household they were astonished because I was well-mannered. I did not portray the traditional bastard mentality. The traditional bastard mentality is seen when someone is downright unruly and rebellious, a renegade so to speak. I, on the other hand, was adorned with accolades and honors: I was a leader in my own right.

I was considered a role model at an early age. My mentality was I could do things on my own. I did not need anybody. Now I would let people help me but when their opinion contradicted my own, I quickly let them know they were not needed for my survival.

This aspect of the bastard mentality is not seen as a bad thing. As a matter of fact, people are praised for being able to have made something out of their lives even though they did not have a father figure. By the world's standards, I should have been put on a pedestal for others to see because of my accomplishments.

However, even though I had many marvelous feats in life being on my own, there were some mistakes I have made. I made the mistakes because the decisions I made were the best I could based upon the knowledge I had. Furthermore, I had an attitude of proving people wrong when some would try to give me advice.

Now the decisions that I made right far exceeded the decisions that I made that were wrong, so I always trusted my judgment. Needless to say, I was not fond of chastisement. After all, I had done so well by myself, who was anybody to tell me the decision I would make was wrong. Even though incognito, this was my bastard mentality.

However, this mentality (no matter how subtle) was not going to be beneficial to me if I was to operate in the Kingdom of God.

What God essentially told me was if I was to be *His* son, then I had to do things *His* way. If I did not, then I was no longer a *son*, but a *bastard*. A son has an inheritance but a bastard is not an heir of anything (Hebrews 12:8). As we saw in the last chapter, Isaac, Abraham's son, received all that Abraham had at the time of his father's death. It was his inheritance.

Ishmael, who was also Abraham's son, only received a gift (Genesis 25:6). Why? Because Ishmael was considered a bastard. If I were to receive my inheritance from God I would have to learn to allow chastisement in my life. One day I was tried in this area and when that trial came, I was a recipient of a rude awakening in life.

Now imagine you have a successful life and someone tells you to stop what you are doing and follow him or her. This is want God asked me. There were dreams I was well on my way to accomplishing when God asked me to submit myself to His leadership. He wanted me to follow after His vision and, for now, leave mine to the side.

With me being a natural leader who had a proven track record, my pride entered in and I said, "*No!*" I resisted God's will for my life for a long time. I had faith in my ability. Furthermore, I saw all the doors opening and favor was coming my way left and right. All I had to do was receive. The path seemed to be made and I was definitely going to walk therein.

Except for one thing, I knew what God wanted me to do. In teaching me how to be a son, He wanted to teach me how to be a servant (Matthew 23:11).

From reading earlier, we know man is supposed to dominate. However, God never intended for us to dominate each other. God only said man should dominate over creatures, or species. What Jesus is telling us is that in order to be great we must learn to serve. Jesus taught His disciples on a consistent basis how to serve others. Even before Jesus was betrayed by Judas, He acted as a servant and washed Judas' feet and the feet of the other eleven disciples (John 13:1-5). The bastard mentality, on the other hand, says that people should be serving me.

We hear this concept of bastard being used all the time on the job. When someone who is a supervisor or has a titled position is considered a hard taskmaster, that person is considered to be a bastard by his or her subordinates. No one likes a bastard. *(I know the word bastard is a dirty word but unless we identify it and attack its characteristics, not the person, this mentality will continue to plague our society).* Let us see an example of this from the Bible.

In 1 Kings 12:3, 4, we learn about King Solomon's son, Rehoboam. King Solomon has died and his son, Rehoboam, begins to reign in his stead. The people of Israel, behind the leading of Jeroboam, went to him and asked him to be more lenient than his father. At this point, Rehoboam can either listen to the people or he can refuse to hear their plea. Before he makes a decision, Rehoboam talks to the same people who counseled his father, Solomon, who was considered the wisest man on the face of the Earth.

You would think he would listen to the counsel of such wise men who sat under the counsel of his father, but he did not. Instead, he goes and talks to his friends about it and listens to them. Listen to what he tells the nation (v. 13, 14). He exhibits two characteristics of the bastard mentality: 1) he refused wise counsel, and 2) he gave in to pressure from peers who have never had any experience in giving advice.

Likewise, so many of our youth today exhibit these same characteristics. They have the attitude of *I can do what I want to*. This is the attitude Rehoboam had. As a ruler, if you have this attitude you will not have many people following you for long. That is exactly what happened in this case. Not only did the people hate him, but he lost ten of the twelve tribes of Israel to Jeroboam.

Even as a leader, God expects you to submit to the people and He expects the people to submit to you. In doing so, order is preserved. God is interested in developing leaders, but not just any leader, a Godlike leader. And guess what? It starts by being a father. A man who cannot lead his own household will never be promoted by God (1 Timothy 3:4, 5).

Learning how to submit, even under harsh circumstances, removes the bastard mentality from you. Furthermore, you will then know how not to treat people as a superior, and because you know this, it makes you a prime candidate for promotion in the eyes of God. When God decides to use somebody, one characteristic He looks for is a person who knows how to deal with people. Why? Because we are all God's children. A father, pastor, business owner or anyone who is in authority will be held accountable for how they treat the people of God (Ephesians 6:9).

Even as leaders, we must do unto others as we want them to do unto us. If we want the people who serve us to submit to us, we must in turn submit ourselves to them. We cannot force people into doing what we want. We must get rid of this mentality if we are to see the sum total blessing of God manifest in our lives.

Developing the Fruit of His Spirit

God will never promote someone who feels they are God's gift to the world. God's gift to the world was Jesus and He is still to return. Since we are not Jesus, we are not God's gift to the world. However, as sons, we do represent God to the world, and God wants us to do so in such a way that people are drawn to Him through our character.

Therefore, we must allow His characteristics to flow in and through us to the world. The characteristics of God are known as the fruit of the Spirit. God wanted to develop in me, as His son, the fruit of His Spirit so I would be able to deal with people in a respectable manner.

The fruit of the Spirit are identified in Galatians 5:22, 23. There are nine characteristics identified as being the fruit of the Spirit, which are: love, joy, peace, longsuffering, gentleness, goodness, faith [faithfulness], meekness and temperance. There is no law against having these characteristics in your life. I want you to notice the characteristics of God are all positive attributes. This should tell you that God is not a negative God and anyone portraying anything negative is not portraying the characteristics of God in their lives.

Now a person can be saved and not yet fully developed in these areas; however, they should continue to strive for mastery of these areas in their lives. Remember, God said through Paul that the son does not receive his inheritance until an appointed time (Galatians 4:1–4). That time is when the person becomes fully developed.

God divided them into three categories to help me understand them and how they should apply to me. All nine of these qualities were key to recreating me in His image. The first category of three deals with how you interact with God. They are love, joy and peace. The second category of three deals with how you interact with your flesh. They are longsuffering, meekness and temperance. The third category of three deals with how you interact with others. They are gentleness, goodness and faith (or faithfulness).

Love, Joy & Peace

As stated, the first category includes love, joy, and peace. These qualities deal with how you interact with God. Furthermore, what God had to get me to realize is that these traits and characteristics originate from Him and must be found from within. In other words, in order for you to have love, joy and peace, you must first accept Jesus into your life.

Once you have done that, you must then have constant fellowship with Him. The more fellowship you have with God, the more these traits of God's character will be developed within you. They cannot be found in things, places, and definitely not people. They can only be found in God. Let us see some scriptures to validate this fact.

Love (1 John 4:16). God is *Love*. Love is the ability to appreciate God, yourself, and others. The only way you can find true love is to have God inside of you. Furthermore, love is about giving, not receiving. A lot of people say they are in love, but they are not. When you are looking to someone else so you can have love, you are wishing to consume what he or she can offer you in the flesh. The word consume denotes that you are receiving something into you. There is no way you can consume and give at the same time.

When a person is experiencing lust, they are seeking to receive something to fill a void. That void must be filled from within. By having love continuously fill you up, you will begin to have an overflow of love. Once you gain that overflow, the love flows out of you and into others. Now, you are in love because you are giving. You are being just like God.

Remember, God so loved the world that He gave His Son (John 3:16). He did this out of compassion. When you truly love, you will be moved out of compassion to help others. You will want to be a servant, serving in any capacity possible. That is what God wants us to do, serve one another. People should be able to see our love for one another and be able to tell we are

Christians (John 13:35). Not only will people see your love, but they will know it is real. People will be drawn to Christ through our love for our brothers and sisters in Christ, as well as others.

Joy (Nehemiah 8:10). Joy is the ability to enjoy happiness. Many people go through life defeated because they do not have the strength to make it. They are plagued with sorrow. They are confronted with trials and tribulations. They see themselves as being victims because they do not have the strength to overcome what they are going through. What they need to understand is the *Joy of the Lord is your strength.*

This joy is not the kind of joy we are used to. This joy comes from knowing that if the LORD is on your side what can man do to you (Psalm 118:6). The only way that you can know God is with you is by the fact that He has to be in you. When you know God is in you and that whatever comes your way you will have the victory, you will have joy.

If you look at this life and take notice of the trials and tribulations, your joy will come when things are going good and leave when things are going bad. But, when you have the Greater One inside you, you will have all the joy in the world because you know you win (*every time!*).

Furthermore, when that joy has bubbled up inside of you, it will begin to flow into the lives of all those with whom you may encounter. When you have joy, God can use you to cause others to have joy. That is how we are to help bear each other's burdens; by lifting the burden with the spirit of joy. You should be filled with so much joy that when you encounter someone whose spirit is down, just being in your presence lifts his or her spirit. Why? Because you have the joy of the LORD inside of you, and that person will be drawn to the joy of the LORD within you. This will also present you with a good witnessing tool. You can help others to realize that the joy you have, they can have it too. Not only that, but they do not have to go through you to get it, they can go to the same place you go to get it, which is the presence of God (Psalm 16:11).

Peace (John 14:27). Peace is the ability to have tranquility in the time of a storm. One of the biggest issues in this world is being faced with trials, tribulations, persecutions and other woes. These everyday problems in life cause us to fall into anxiety, worry, frustration and anger. Trust me, everyone has felt this way before and no one likes it.

You hear people say that they need to do something in order to get something else off their mind. Why? They do not have any peace so they go searching for it. People who do not know Christ seek for it in the world. They do things for the simple fact of easing their mind. These include drinking their problems away, smoking to calm their nerves, using drugs to give them a high, and other things, which can only give them temporary relief.

But, when you as a son of God, have peace, one of the fruit of the Spirit, residing inside you, you don't have to rely on external elements to rectify an internal problem. The peace of God will keep you even while going through the harshest of situations. People will look at you and wonder *how in the world you made it through when other people going through the same problem couldn't make it?*

As a son of God, we have a promise of receiving peace that passes all natural knowledge and understanding (Philippians 4:7). When the world sees this peace, they will want it. It is what this world is in need of. Every one is searching for it and as a son of God you have the privilege of having it. It is in you, but you must allow God to develop it.

Now these three qualities are tools by which you can draw others to Christ. The world is in dire need of something, but they do not know what it is. However, they should be able to see a son of God and say, *"They have what I am looking for."*

The world is waiting for us to be manifested (Romans 8:19). Why? The love, joy, and peace of God cannot flow from God into them except they receive Him. However, the love, joy, and peace of God can flow through His sons (and daughters) into the lives of other people. When this happens, people become drawn to us as sons, in which we, as sons, can now lead them to Christ.

These three qualities are God's way of flowing into this world, but it will only happen if the Christian has developed in these areas. Many Christians have not been developed in these areas and that is why many people in the world are not drawn to Christ. Why? We represent Him to the world. If they do not see love, joy, and peace in us, they will not see it in Him. Growing up without a father can definitely deplete and take away these characteristics in a person's life, but God can and will restore them if you allow Him to. He did it for me and He will do it for you.

Longsuffering, Meekness & Temperance

These three traits of the fruit of the Spirit are in the second category that deals with how we interact with our flesh. The first three basically dealt with the edifying of our spirit, or inner being. These three deal with the mortifying of our flesh. The first three can only come from God. These three can only come from us. We have to make a decision as well as put forth concerted effort in order to flow in these traits. However, do not misunderstand me; we will not be able to flow in these three areas if we do not develop in the other three areas *first*.

Longsuffering (1 Timothy 1:16). Longsuffering is the ability to endure through trials. In the context of this Scripture, Paul is telling Timothy, that being a pattern and an example to others, he should allow longsuffering to be seen in his life as he encounters the attacks of the Devil. Longsuffering simply means patient endurance. This covers dealing with people and dealing with situations. In either case, our flesh does not like to feel uncomfortable.

There may be people who get on your last nerve and you do not like being around them; however, for whatever reason we have to interact with them. In this case, we have to forbear them in love (but if we do not have love, we will not forbear). When the person we are dealing with sees that we are forbearing their actions in love, they will begin to change their actions towards us. Longsuffering causes us to deal with the action and still love the person. Trust me, this must be developed and it will not be easy. Yet, by you allowing God to be seen through us, people will be drawn to Him.

Other times, we may be in a situation that is uncomfortable, yet we know we have to go through this in order to get to the other side, and because we know this, we patiently endure. For example, some students dread going to school because it challenges them beyond their current capability. So what do they do? They do not even try, cut class or even drop out because it gets hard. This mentality has caused many to just give up.

However, my friend, we live in a hot world and if we want to eat, we are going to have to go to somebody's kitchen. We have to be able to bear up under intense conditions. It may be painful, but this is a characteristic that we must develop. Developing this quality proves our faith in God, and a *son should also know his Father will see him through because of the love that God has in and towards him* (1 Corinthians 13:7).

Meekness (Colossians 3:12). As the elect of God, meaning we are a sons and daughters, meekness is a quality we should have. Meekness is simply the act of knowing who we are without promoting it to others. It is the very opposite of something called pride. Pride puffs up itself, promotes itself, and challenges any one who would come up against itself. With pride, it is all about self.

Meekness, on the other hand, looks for ways to serve others, to make sure others are comfortable, and does not show anger when attacked. I am not saying we will not get angry, but we should look at the situation and say, *"I take down and humble myself so that the situation will end in peace."* Meekness is seeing someone as our equal yet preferring that person above ourselves. People do not like to be meek because they oftentimes get taken advantage of. It is not God's will for this to happen; but it does. What we should realize is that just as people take advantage of God, they will take advantage of us. The world's mindset is thinking how people can be a help to *me*. As children of God, we should have the mind of Christ, which says, it is all about how we can be a help to others.

Because we have this mindset, people will try to take advantage of us; however, we also know that if someone takes advantage of us, they will have to deal with our Heavenly Father. In one situation in my life, I made a mistake of trying to deal with the situation myself. God told me to hold my peace and let Him fight my battle, but my sentiments were, *"No, they have crossed over their boundaries and I am going to deal with it."* And I did, but in doing so I lost out on something that was very precious to me.

People may take advantage of you but by your continuing to be humble before God, He will exalt you in due season (1 Peter 5:6). In some cases, God will cause that person to see their wrong and change. In other cases, God will cause that person to become your footstool. Either way, you will have the victory. God will protect the meek.

If you read Numbers 12, you will see the context of the story of Moses, who was known as a very meek man. Miriam and Aaron, Moses' sister and brother, were in strife over the fact they felt that Moses should have married someone else; therefore, they murmured against him. God called Moses and He equipped Moses to do the task He called Moses to do. They were not mad about the job Moses was doing; they only had a problem with whom he was married to.

When you are meek, people will tend to tell you what you should and should not be doing. It is okay for people to give you advice but they are stepping over the line when they try to force it on you. In this case, God will deal with them in a like manner that He dealt with Miriam and Aaron. God is on your side, but you have to have faith in Him in order to operate in the spirit of meekness. If not, you will be fighting your own battles, in which you will never win. But with God, you win every time. The only battle you will have to fight is the one with your flesh.

Temperance (1 Corinthians 9:25). This trait is also closely related to patiently enduring, humility and the denial of the flesh. In a nutshell, temperance is simply self-discipline, which is enduring short-term suffering in your flesh to enjoy long-term gain in your life. The flesh says, *I want it now*, and an undisciplined person will feed the hunger of their flesh. Without this quality of temperance, mankind would utterly destroy itself.

Temperance keeps anger from becoming wrath and wrath from becoming murder. Temperance keeps passion from turning into lust and lust into fornication. Temperance keeps hunger from turning into compulsive eating and that into obesity. Temperance is what causes you to not respond to someone when they have disrespected you in such a way that just makes your blood boil.

Temperance is an operative of love. By being well tempered, you will not lash out at people over big, as well as little, issues. You may get angry, but your anger will not lead you to sin (Ephesians 4:26). The love inside of you will cause you to release the anger, instead of holding on to it.

Temperance is an operative of joy. The person who operates in temperance knows, whatever the situation is, no external thing can take away their joy. Because of this, that kind of person is not easily depressed because their joy is not in things.

Temperance is an operative of patience. Temperance will cause you to delay your self-gratification because you know if you hold off on receiving this *"must have"*, you will gain control over your flesh. By operating in this characteristic, you will not rush into something that may cause you to later regret.

Self-discipline is an area many people do not operate in. Because of this, many encounter problems that could have otherwise been avoided. For example, a person who is not temperate in their eating causes them to operate in the sin of gluttony (overeating). Due to their gluttonous actions, they become overweight and encounter health problems they otherwise would not have encountered.

Likewise in our spending, if we do not use temperance in our finances we will incur debt that goes beyond our ability to repay, which is sin (Romans 13:8). Temperance causes us to be content and not get over into the area of *overdoing it*. Without temperance, we will operate in a mentality that says, *go for it*, and, *if you feel like doing it, then do it*. However, by being temperate you are letting God know you trust Him and His timing. It is also a step of faith because you will not be weary in well-doing (Galatians 6:9).

As you can see, these three characteristics of God can greatly benefit mankind. The opposite of longsuffering, meekness, and temperance are wrath and indignation, pride and lasciviousness (the "feel good" mentality). Can you image what the world would look like if the latter characteristics ran freely in society? If you are honest, you are thinking to yourself that the world you are imagining pretty much resembles certain parts of the world today. When God told me He would recreate me in His image, these are definitely traits and qualities He wants me, as well as all the rest of His children, to have.

Gentleness, Goodness and Faith (Faithfulness)

These three traits of the fruit of the Spirit are in the third category, which deals with how you interact with other people. How you treat people will carry you a long way. Knowing how to treat and interact with people will cause you to be promoted and preferred above others who may be more qualified than you, but they lack having good people skills. When you begin to operate in these characteristics, you are beginning to take upon yourself the qualities of being a leader. When you exhibit good leadership characteristics, people will follow you. Some leaders, even though they are not godly, have large followings because they operate and flow in these traits. The world calls it charisma. *However, please note the best leader is often times a great friend.*

Gentleness (Ephesians 4:32). This interpretation of the word gentleness comes from the Greek word *"chrestotes"*, which can be translated gentleness, kindness, and tenderness. As children of God, He wants us to have this characteristic. There are many families that have love toward each other; they just do not have gentleness. Everyone is yelling and fussing and fighting. No one has any kind words to say to the other. They are always telling each other off.

They do love each other; they just do not know how to show it. Everyone is so rough and coarse with each other that the other person does not feel the love even though it is there. Trust me: we need this characteristic of gentleness.

The Bible says a soft answer turns away wrath (Proverbs 15:1). We need to learn to deal kindly with each other. Sometimes best friendships are severed forever because we do not know how to deal kindly with each other. However, the spirit of gentleness will cause you to be able to reach even those whom you have hurt.

A gentle person knows that someone is hurting and that the person must be dealt with delicately. A gentle spirit will allow you to cry with those who cry and rejoice with those who rejoice. It is simply compassion. Compassion will cause you to look at someone who has messed up and say, "*I want to help you. I am on your side. Whatever you need, just call.*" This characteristic lets a person know you genuinely care for them.

This characteristic will also allow you to deal kindly with people who may have hurt you. Many see this as a form of weakness; therefore, they lash out in anger and wrath. However, having a gentle spirit will cause you to handle the situation with care and respect for the other person. In 1 Samuel 18:14, it talks about how David *behaved himself wisely.* Now King Saul was trying to kill him (in verse 11, he threw a javelin at David). Yet David treated him with respect.

Having a gentle spirit will cause you to not act on the revenge you want to give out. Our mindset today is *I am going to get you before you get me.* No one is being gentle in the situation. *But my feelings got hurt.* We all get hurt but that does not mean we should take revenge. The Bible tells us that with gentleness (loving kindness) God drew us to Him (Jeremiah 31:3). This is how we will draw others to us, even those who have hurt us. Why? We should do even as Christ did when He hung on the Cross, He said, *"Father, forgive them for they know not what they do"* (Luke 23:34).

This characteristic of gentleness is a combination of all the previous six qualities. You need love to forgive and have compassion. You need joy because trying times can and will cause you to act out of character. You need peace so that you can weather the storm without being swayed. You need longsuffering because people will try you. You need meekness because everyone wants to be right and someone needs to say to themselves, *this argument is not worth losing our friendship.* And finally, you need temperance because if you do not know how to control your emotions, they will get the best of you.

Goodness (Ephesians 5:9-11). When most people see this word, they automatically think it simply means being a good person; however, to truly understand this word we must utilize the original Greek text to see what characteristic it denotes. This rendering of the word *"goodness"* comes from the Greek word *"agathosune,"* which means to do good to others in a way that is not considered gentle, but stern.

Too many times we like our friends to be sympathetic to our needs, situations, and sorrows. We want to act like babies and have our friends breast feed us until we feel better. We exhibit this *"woe is me"* attitude and a *"nobody knows the trouble I see but Jesus"* mentality, and when we go to friends we want them to pamper our sorrows. If they do not, we think, *I thought they were my friends; and if so, why don't they feel sorry for me.*

A friend that would let you have a pity-party is allowing you to produce in your life unfruitful works of darkness. It is unfruitful because pouting never solves anything. It is darkness because you cannot see that you are more than a conqueror. The best kind of friend you could have would tell you (about your sorrows), *"Get over it!"*

A good friend is not going to allow you to wallow in your sorrows; yet, they will pump you up into believing you can and will get over them. A good friend reminds you that you were somebody before you started going through this situation, you have the strength to go through this situation and you have the perseverance to make it out of this situation. A good friend will drag you out of your pit of doom and gloom even if you want to stay there. *This type of friend becomes your greatest cheerleader in your lowest hour.*

This term "goodness" also means that if you are going in the wrong direction, they will tell you, and because of their concern for you, they will also tell you of any imperfections they see in your ways. Too many times we want a cheerleader to cheer us on even though we are going in the wrong direction. However, it is in the characteristic of a good friend that he or she *will reprove your ways* (note: they are not reproving you but your ways). But we do not want that.

We want friends who will agree with what we are thinking and we shun those who do not. *This is the friend we yell at and fuss with because their opinion is contrary to what we want and that is selfish.* And even though we totally disrespect them, they are still there trying to help steer us in the right direction. Why? Because they love us.

Most people just like to give their opinion about everything. What they do is either out of pride (trying to pass themselves off as if they give great wisdom) or it is self-motivated (they want you to do something that will benefit them). How can you tell if they are portraying the characteristic of goodness? Goodness will also be accompanied and balanced with gentleness.

A friend will be gentle with you because they do not want to hurt your feelings. A friend will be good to you because they do not want to see you get hurt by doing something that is not constructive to your life. These two must be well-balanced, or you will have a friend that always goes along with what you are doing, or one that you always argue with that eventually terminates the friendship. A true friend knows when to be gentle and when to be good. We like our gentle friends, but we definitely need our good ones.

This balance of characteristics reminds me of my grandmother. She was so gentle and kind toward me. I remember she used to call me over, give me some cookies and milk, and talk to me about how much she loved me. She would bring out the Word of God and expound on how He loved me even more. She used to say, *"If I could take the Word and pour it into your head I would. But since I can't I will just teach it to you."*

That was grandma. She just had a gentle spirit, always hospitable. She beat me at times and when she finished, she would sit me back down and let me know she loved me and did not want anything bad to happen to me. Trust me, I did not like the beating, but I loved her for it. Why? Because she gave me gentleness and goodness in a balanced way. She reproved me in what actions I may have taken, but then she would gently lead me in the right direction.

It was good that my grandmother had this quality, but it is one that I should have received from my father.

Faith (faithfulness) (Proverbs 27:6). A pastor of a church I attended while in college told me a friend is someone who knows something about you that could destroy you, but because they are your friend, they do not disclose it. God is interested in people being faithful to others even if they are not faithful to you. In doing so, we show ourselves to be conforming to the image of Christ. In Romans 5:8, it tells us Christ died for us even though we lived contrary to God. Why? Because He is faithful. Not only that, God forgives us to the point of never remembering it nor ever bringing it back up. (1 John 1:9).

God is faithful to us and He wants us to be faithful to each other. Why is God faithful to us? He is dedicated to our becoming His children. He loves us so much that He is willing to put up with our imperfections just to have fellowship with us. He will never leave us, nor will He ever forsake us (Hebrews 13:5). If we make our beds in Hades, God would still be there for us according to Psalm 139:8. Even though the word *"Hades"* is referring to the place of the dead, God's presence spans all places in between.

We can be heading on our way to Hades but God's grace and mercy will stop us from reaching there because God is faithful. There is a saying, *God is good all the time and all the time God is good.* Why is God good? Because He is faithful. Too many times we do not want to put up with people's imperfect ways and when things get too rough and too heated, we leave that person because we do not want to deal with them nor their issues. We are not faithful to them. A lot of times people know they have issues; however, they do not know how to change. A faithful friend will work with them in helping them to change and they will continue to be there despite the fact of whether the person changes or not. I learned a valuable lesson in that if you put up with a person's worst, they, in turn, will give you their best.

This is often the case with youth who have been labeled as delinquents. Many times when they come into contact with authority figures they rebel because no one has ever been faithful to them. They always receive harsh criticism when they do something wrong. I am not saying that one should not receive chastisement, but I am saying before someone will receive chastisement from you they need to know you will be faithful to them. Goodness and gentleness combined with faithfulness is needed to bring about change.

I remember teaching a technical math class at C.A. Johnson High School in Columbia, SC. This class was basically filled with students labeled as remedial and they acted that way because of how they were labeled. They told me in my first week of teaching, *"Mr. Wilson, you teach too fast. You need to slow down. Didn't they tell you when they hired you that this is the remedial class? That means we are SLOW!"* After hearing that I thought to myself, *what in the world have I gotten myself into?* It was not that they could not learn: they just did not want to.

Regardless of what they said, I pushed them past their limits and got them to think outside of the box they had placed themselves in. I did not accept their excuses and I did not allow them to either. By me doing this, I met a lot of resistance from them, because when a person is trying their best and they fall short, frustration sets in. When that happens, a person will lash out at the one causing them the frustration, which in this case was me. There were many times I wanted to quit, and many times they felt my anger, (even though I did not say anything to them) because of their rebellion. They were frustrated with me and I was frustrated with them.

One time I got really angry and one of my students said, *"Mr. Wilson, are you angry with us?"* I gave no reply. They

Re-created in the Image of My Heavenly Father

continued, *"I bet you are going to do just like everyone else and give up on us."* By this time I realized these kids had never had any one be as faithful to them as I was. So you know what I did? I gave them my best and put up with their worst.

There was not one student in there that did not (at one point in time) succeed in passing either an assignment or a test. Some of them even changed their whole attitude and turned out to be the smartest in the class. By the time I left that class, each student knew in their hearts they could do the work if they only tried. However, they did not have many people like me in their lives, so after I left they reverted back to their old ways. Most people are not self-motivated and before you can be faithful to others, you have to be faithful to yourself.

Those kids loved me and they showed it in the strangest ways. There was this one guy who wanted me to spend time teaching him during my free time and he had me thinking he was giving up gym class for math. I thought to myself, *I am really making a difference in his life.* Here he is giving up gym for math (even when I was in school it was the other way around). I was so proud of him. Then one day the principal came down to my room with him.

I found out later he was skipping his English class to go to the gym, so he really was not leaving his gym class for mine, but his English class. As I was being told this, I looked at him and all he could do was hang his head down. I could see he was trying not to burst out in laughter, and if the truth be told, I was trying to do the same. And even though what he did was wrong, I was proud (not at his wrongdoing) at the tenacity he showed in wanting to learn what I was teaching. I thought to myself, *what if everyone in his life would take the time and effort to teach and reach him the way I did.*

There was this girl in my class who was rough around the edges; always had something smart to say and always telling someone off. When I first came to that class, she would not do anything. She would disrupt the class just to be disruptive.

James 3:16 says that where strife and envying is, there will be found confusion and every evil work. Well, strife and envy must have been her two middle names. She was always trying to find a reason to *bust somebody in the mouth*. She challenged me quite a few times but I did not back down.

The students looked at my age and had a hard time respecting me because I was so young. She was one of the toughest but I stuck with her. By the time that year was over, she had the highest GPA in the class. In my class, she became an A student. I was even privileged to see her compassionate side because she felt comfortable enough to let her guard down in my class. Come to find out, this grizzly bear was nothing more than a teddy bear who needed someone to be faithful to her and stick with her no matter what.

That is what they all wanted and that is what I did my best to give them. You will reap what you sow. By me giving them faithfulness, they in turn gave faithfulness back to me (at least some of them). The ones that did not do well in my class were not motivated enough to be self-disciplined to do the work. In other words, they were not faithful to themselves.

In life, it is good to have people who are faithful to you; however, if you are not faithful to yourself you will not make it in this world. People come and go, but self-motivation comes from within.

God Wants to Build Character

Love. Joy. Peace. Longsuffering. Gentleness. Goodness. Faith. Meekness. Temperance. All these qualities are traits and characteristics that God wants to build inside of you. He wants to recreate your sinful nature from being all about what others can do for you to a god-like nature of what you can do for others. When we allow God to build these qualities within us, we are allowing Him to transform us into the image of His dear Son, Jesus Christ.

Now you may be saying to yourself *these are HIGH standards*. Guess what? They are. Guess why? Because we are children of the most high God. And as such, the standards will be high. Can you do it on your own? No. The only way you can attain such high standards in your life is by the help of God.

John 1:12 states: *"But as many as received him, to them gave he power to become the sons of God, even to them that believe on His name."*

How do you get this power? Acts 1:8 states*: "But ye shall receive power, after that the Holy Ghost is come upon you: and ye shall be witnesses unto Me both in Jerusalem, and in all Judaea, and in Samaria, and unto the uttermost part of the earth."*

God wants to equip you with His power to become His children. He is going to give you power to witness that Jesus is the Christ. And the greatest witness one could have is the life they live. God wants your life to be a witness of Christ unto Him, your Father.

Do You See the Fear

Do you see the fear in my eyes,
Disguising myself with lies,
Pretending to be
Someone who's not really me.

Living life like I know what's true,
Yet I don't have a clue what in this life I am to do,
So I allow myself to flow
With the currents of life,
As I fight this unwanted fight,
Trying to discern between what's wrong and what's right,
That I might be righteous in my own eyes.

Yet through the same eyes that I see righteous,
I wonder do you see my fear,
Don't draw near
Or you might see the real me.

It's a dog-eat-dog life
And you gotta scrap for every bite,
Just to survive that's true,
But sometimes you gotta do what you gotta do.
But if I only knew
How to break this cycle.

Just to be real
So I can feel the quietness of my soul,
To make my emotion stilled
From these escapades of life,
Fighting off all this bitterness and strife
That surrounds me.
Drowning myself in tears
Because all these years
I still haven't faced my fears.

There's the fear of not having succeeded;
Of not being loved; of not being needed;
The fear that all my labor is in vain;
And at the end of the day, no one will know my name.

So I succeed at nothing,
Won't give myself to love,
I need no man, and
I'm known for all the wrong reasons.
Surrounded by shame,
No one will ever forget my name.

Yeah, they see my blaze
As I grace and amaze them with my style,
But I wonder do they see my fear,
Don't draw near,
Or you might see
The real me.

Chapter 5

Masking It

The Silent Voice

Unheard, I scream all day,
Unnoticed, I set my actions ablaze,
Misunderstand, I defy sense,
Denied, I force my way out,
Longing, I give myself to love,
Unwanted, I live in isolation,
Forgotten, I become a silent voice.
My tears go unnoticed,
My moans are silenced,
No empathy for me,
One door,
No key.

Inside–Out

While growing up I was the man of the house. Because of this, I felt I had to be strong for the women in the house. I remember when it used to thunder and storm at night my sister would run into my mother's room because she was afraid. Then I would come in the room and my sister would say, *"Are you scared too?"* I replied in my manly adolescent voice, *"No, I'm just here to make sure that ya'll are alright. Now move over and make room for me."* Was I scared? You better believe it (up until a certain age). Was I going to let them see it? No, so I had to mask it.

Masking it was my way of proving I was the man of the house. As the "Big" little man of the house, I thought it was beneath me to show fear or emotion. (Besides, the women in the house already did that). I felt they were going to look to me for strength. And as time would have it, they did.

When I got older, my sister would begin to come and talk to me about different issues and problems in her life. She truly valued my advice. If a man was not acting right, she talked to me about it. If a friend of hers began acting like a fool, she talked to me about it. If she and mom had an intense time of fellowship, she talked to me. Not only did she talk to me, but my mom talked to me as well. It got to the point that when they got into a heated discussion, one would call me and ask if I had talked to the other one yet. If not, they would proceed with their side of the story. If I had, they would ask me what the other one said. What I started doing was telling them I did not know anything. That way I could give them good advice without them thinking I was biased. However, they thought that anyway.

I would tell each of them what they needed to do in order to heal the relationship. They did not want to hear that. They wanted me to talk to the other about what they wanted the other person to do. When I would not, both would say, *"You are just taking her side."* That was the farthest thing from the truth. I loved both of them and wanted them to work on their side of the relationship. Convincing them of that is a book entirely by itself.

Masking It

Even though they came to me with their problems, I did not do the same. My mom said she was concerned about me growing up because I did not talk about my issues. I always kept to myself and she did not know how to reach me. There are so many children out there going through the same thing. They are not opening up to their parents and the parents do not know how to reach them. Like my mom, the parents can only hope there is nothing wrong with their child.

Children sometimes mask their fears for many different reasons. In my case, I wanted to show everyone how strong I was and how much I could take. In other cases, a child may be afraid of how that parent is going to react. Sometimes, the child does not open up because there is no trust between the child and the parent. Trust must be established at an early age if the lines of communication are going to be open. Other times, even though the parent and the child live under the same roof, they do not know each other. This essentially means they do not have a relationship.

Children need to know they have a support and backing to fall back on. If not, they will come home and pretend like everything is all right, even though they are hurting. They are to be nourished, which means to promote the growth of. Part of promoting the growth of a child is protecting them from things that will potentially hinder their growth.

I remember my sister and mother getting into heated discussions over my sister not feeling that my mother protected her from certain elements of life. In my mother's defense, she was only one person and was being stretched in many directions. In most cases my mother did, but she did not do it the way my sister wanted her to. In other cases, my mother did not, because it was not a job she was equipped to do. It was a job my father should have been there to do.

Regardless, that issue between my sister and mother led to many discussions and the flaring of many emotions. They loved each other to life; however, so much pain was caused by the divorce that they used each other as an outlet. Do not get me wrong; we had a very loving family. It was just at times, we did not know how to communicate our true feelings, and instead of dealing with them appropriately, we would mask it.

So many times we only deal with the pain and not the issue. That, my friend, is masking it. We go on with life pretending everything is okay. On the outside we seem fine, but on the inside we are burning wood chips. In life, people will hurt us and we also hurt others. Sometimes we will hurt others with the best of "our" intentions (I say "our" because most of the time we think of how we want things done). However, we need to understand our way is not the only way nor is it always the best way for others.

Temporary Insanity

A lot of times when we are hurting and want to get away from the pain, we go and do something senseless. Why? Because it feels good and we will do anything to forget the pain. That is why most women go shopping after they experience something real dramatic. By buying an outfit that looks good, no matter how expensive it is, it gives them a temporary sense of satisfaction.

When some men get mad, they go for a ride and usually drive at an excessive speed. We see it all the time in other people, and strangely enough, other people see it in us. We sometimes even see it in ourselves. Then we think: *why did I do that?* I will tell you why. *It felt good!*

I remember while I was in college I experienced this thing called Temporary Insanity. Basically, I grew up in church all my life. I did not know a lot about partying, clubbing and the like. My mother did not want me to live that kind of lifestyle. However, during college I became frustrated with class assignments, deadlines for projects, and to top it off, my girlfriend was cheating on me. I felt like I was going to lose it.

Masking It

So what did I do? I started wilding out (for those of you who do not understand this terminology, it means to act crazy).

One time, my friends were playing Master P's hit, *No Limit Soldier*. When they would do this they would be out in the hallway jumping around, moving and grooving to the beat while I usually stayed in my room. But that day, something came over me (and it was not the Holy Ghost and His quickening power).

I came out of my room and began to dance and yell the song out just like they were. If you did not know me, you would have thought I was a natural. But because my frat brothers knew me, they looked at me as if to say, *Terrence has lost his mind and is going crazy. Someone call 911, quick.* Ohhh, it felt GOOD. Was it good for my spirit? *Yeah right.* Was it good to my flesh? *Oh yeah.*

I jumped myself tired. I took a nap and woke up only to find the problems were still there. I think back to some of the things I did and just laugh because I realize I was temporarily insane to have even thought doing those things would have made me feel any better.

We do things to experience a rush of adrenaline and it causes us to feel powerful. We are no longer the victim. So, guess what? We do it again. And again. And again. And again. The next thing you know we have made a lifestyle of doing things that gives us a rush. Now our temporary insanity has become a lifestyle of being permanently insane. Only this lifestyle is filled with drugs, promiscuous sex, drunkenness, lasciviousness and other things that satisfy the flesh.

In some cases, we even begin to victimize others. The same pain others have made us feel we, in turn, oppress another person with the same circumstance. The bad thing about it is we accept the excuse *this is who I am*. We *do not* understand we can become children of the Most High God, thereby, taking upon us His character. We do not know who we were made to be by the Most High. We only accept who we are, which is based upon who we have been made to be, due to the circumstances of our lives.

I remember another time I purposely did not do an assignment because of the pressure I was faced with. I began to skip class. My thought was, *life is not supposed to be this hard; therefore, I am going to make it easier on myself by doing things that will not cause me to be challenged. And every time I run into a problem I will just avoid it. And if things get too tough, I'll just enter the realm of temporary insanity to deal with it and every thing will be all right. Right?*

The truth is we do things that make us void of responsibility. If we do not have any responsibilities then we should not have any worries, right? We do this because we fear failure. We think if we never apply ourselves, we will never fail. I had to realize it is better to fall on your face trying then to not try at all. Nobody wants to be laughed at; however, you find out who your true friends are when you fall. They are the ones who help you back up. They are the ones who encourage you. They are the ones who wrap their arms around you and let you know, not only that you will succeed if you keep trying, but they will love you regardless.

Let me tell you, we need friends like that, but even more importantly, we need fathers like that. We need fathers who will be there to pick us up when we fall, wipe the dust off of us, give us a pat on the behind, and tell us, *"Get back out there because you can do it. You know why you can do it? Because you are my child and that means you are a winner."*

Frustration & Rebellion

We Get Frustrated! Life has its curve balls and we have struck out so many times we feel as if we are failures. Frustration sets in because we do not know where to go from here. Then we begin to see people around us as hindrances. Even though they did nothing to add to the problem, but because they do not seem to help alleviate it we see them as a continuation of the problem.

You may have heard this before, "I am having a bad day and you are not doing anything to help it." Or maybe this one is more familiar, "You are getting on my last nerve!" And you are thinking, I wonder who got on your first nerve because if they did not get on your first nerve, maybe I would not be getting on your last one. Too many times others become the outlet for our frustrations, and too many of those times the targets of our frustrations are our family members, especially our children.

You must understand everyone has dreams and when we cannot see those dreams come to fruition, we begin to force things. We try to force situations that are not there. We place people under unneeded stress and pressure. We say things we should not and do not mean; yet, we say it out of anger because we see ourselves as failing our life's goal. Well, I understand nobody likes to fail but that does not make what we do right.

Too many times we go through life pretending like everything is all right; however, frustration due to life is building on the inside. And instead of dealing with it properly, we mask it. Yet like a balloon being filled with hot air, there is only so much we can hold within before we burst.

When we, as adults, experience pain we do not know how to handle, we take it out on those around us. For example, a husband had a bad day at work and comes home. When he gets there dinner is not ready, so he goes off on a temper tantrum. The wife, who is innocent, is now hurt and seeks for revenge.

So what she does is begin to withhold sexual gratification from her husband. One thing leads to the next and now they are fighting all the time. Why? Because the husband did not have an adequate avenue to release his frustrations, he finds the closest thing, in most cases a person, to release his frustrations on (this is no excuse for his actions).

We must understand children are simply little adults and react the same way. Because they cannot verbalize it, it is expressed through their actions. There are many ways their pain is expressed through their actions, but many parents tend to see it in the form of rebellion. The parent just thinks the child has an attitude problem when the real issue is the child is crying out for someone to water down the burning flame in their soul. Yet, the only thing that tends to happen is the parent adds more fuel to the fire because they do not know how to adequately handle the situation.

Their rebellion is screaming *I hate you*. However, what I have noticed is they are actually trying you to see if you really love them. Because a divorce has occurred, the child already feels it is because the parent loves his or herself more than the child. Internally, they are thinking, *if you love me then you will prove it*. Now there is a way to love a child through chastisement without the child thinking you are mad with them.

I remember while growing up my grandmother would give me spankings. Yet when she did it, she did so with love and tenderness. Maybe not so tender but I knew she loved me. The first thing she would do was call me over to her house to talk. While talking, she would take out her Bible. (Now my grandmother taking out her Bible did not mean anything because she always talked to her grandchildren from the Bible). The way I would know what was going to happen would be based upon the Scripture she would use.

She would say something like, "Terry, let me show you what the Bible says in Proverbs 23:13-14. *Withhold not correction from the child: for if thou beatest him with the rod, he shall not die. Thou shalt beat him with the rod, and shalt deliver his soul from hell.*

"In other words, if you spare the rod, you spoil the child. Now this is gonna hurt me more than it does you, but I'm doing it because I love you. Now go get the switch off of the good tree." Hurt you more than it hurts me? Come on, I was thinking. Then I had to choose which switch I wanted to get whipped with (at least she gave me a choice, some switches

Masking It

were flexible and did not break easily while others did and you know which one I chose). Through the pain I suffered I knew she loved me. My grandmother sat me down more to tell me about the goodness of God than she did to beat me.

I remember the last time my grandmother beat me. She quoted the same Scripture; however, this time she came over to my house and had a belt. She was talking to me as I was sitting in a chair. Soon after, she began to beat me and halfway through she began to cry. But even in crying, in between lashes, she told me, *"I am doing this because I love you."*

I could hear in her voice it really was hurting her more than it hurt me. I was hurting physically, but she was hurting spiritually. I could hear her spirit crying out to God, *I've done the best that I could and it still seems not to have been good enough.* My grandmother was crying because she felt like she failed in helping to raise me to be an asset, first, to God, and also to society.

At that point in my life, I made a decision if someone cared about me that much I have an obligation to make something out of myself. Furthermore, I was reminded of the promise I made to myself at an early age, *when I get older things will be much different. I'm gonna be a man.* Right then I realized that I was on the wrong track and made a decision to change.

Deliberate Rebellion

But at least it was my grandmother doing the beating. I accepted my grandmother's beating but my grandfather was another story. With him, it was his sixty five year old male ego versus my eight-year-old male ego. I probably could write another book on the encounters between my grandfather and myself. I always rebelled against him because I did not feel the same love from him that my grandmother had. Furthermore, my grandfather would say things like, "I'm gonna beat the devil outta you." That only made me rebel more and show him the devil that was in me (Please note: the only devil that I have ever had in me was the old unregenerated person that I used to be. That was the old me and not an evil being that caused me to spit up and throw up green slime. Trust me I was not actually possessed even though at times I may have temporarily acted like it).

I remember the last time my grandfather tried to beat me (remember the wood chip story). He was talking and giving me the same old line about what he was going to do and I would just look at him with eyes of hatred. He kept talking, then he decided he had said enough and it was time for me to get what I had coming to me.

He came within five feet of where I was. I saw a pipe on the ground; I picked it up and swung it at him. For the first time in my life, I saw fear in my grandfather's eyes. It was the very same fear he had previously seen in mine. You must understand two things. First, I was terrified of my grandfather and did what I did out of fear and anger (I make no excuse for what I did). However, when a child is hurting on the inside and lives in fear at the same time, you never know what that child, or adult, might do. Everyone has his or her breaking point, and he had crossed mine. He, along with other situations that had occurred in my life, provoked me to wrath (Ephesians 6:4).

Wrath is anger in action. Whenever you put someone in fear of you or you constantly hound him or her, they will respond in a very unpleasant way. Whether adult or child, they are human (even if they are a Christian, they are still human and we must respect, honor, and remember that). Even in chastising people, whether adult or child, you must do it in love. Even God uses loving-kindness in dealing with us (Jeremiah 31:3).

The second thing you must understand is, if it had not been for the Word of God planted on the inside of me, I would have swung a second time. I may not have been living for God, but the Word of God was in my heart. What I did was out of fear and it was an instantaneous action. It happened without a thought. At that point in my life, I would do things like that.

However, as I developed in the things of God through my Lord and Savior Jesus Christ, the Holy Spirit within developed in me, over time, the fruit of the Spirit. I am not saying I do not get frustrated to the point of action, but the God in me keeps me from doing anything stupid. I John 5:18 states, *". . . but he that is begotten of God keepeth himself, and that wicked one toucheth him not."* I cannot stress enough how much the knowledge of Jesus Christ has kept me on the right path, nor can I stress how much the development of His Spirit on the inside of me has withheld me from going off on others. *If He did it for me, He will do it for you.*

Fear: The Root of It All

I was not going to live in fear anymore. I was going to do what was necessary to make sure people did not hurt me more than I already was. Hurt and pain lead to fear, and fear leads to wrath and anger. I, like most people, do not like to show people I am afraid. So what did I do? I masked it.

We mask things because we feel if people see our fear, they will either expose it or take advantage of it. We believe that people will view it as a weakness, an area they can use against us and attack us. Masking it allows us to pretend we're doing just fine, when we are really in suffering and pain. All this leads to a lack of trust of others, which is a symptom of fear. We especially do not trust people who may have treated us in a way that reminds us of a past hurt.

For example, a woman may pretend everything is okay with her despite the fact she has been raped. However, when a man gets too close to her or approaches her in a way that reminds her of the rape, she has a relapse. She remembers the scenario, thinks the same thing will happen again, and reacts in a way so that she will be able to protect herself. This may even occur with her husband, and if she still lives in fear the two of them will never have the marriage they should because of it. She sets up a wall that even her husband cannot get over.

Likewise, children who have been hurt, sometimes never allow the right person to enter into their hearts because they have a wall of resistance. Yet, as they go about life from day to day, no one can tell until something causes the shaken soda pop bottle to be opened. A shaken soda pop bottle looks no different from one that has not been shaken. You can look at both all you want; you will never be able to tell from the outside what is happening on the inside. The only way to find out is to open it. Just like a shaken bottle, if you get involved with someone who is hurt you get the pleasure of experiencing the explosion. You are thinking to yourself, *where did all this come from? It ain't that deep.* From your standpoint, it may not be, but in their case, it is. You are not the main problem, you are just the one who opened the bottle.

Even though you were the one they exploded on, they look at you and say, *"Okay, you opened me up, now you help me deal with my problem."* You are thinking in the back of your mind, *let me leave them alone.* However, if you do that they see you as someone who really does not care about them, because if you cared about them, you would care enough to help them through their issues. What you have encountered is their front line of defense.

People are like puffer fish. The puffer fish dwells in the deep blue sea with many sea creatures larger than itself. It is near the bottom of the food chain and would be the subject of many attacks if it had not been for its defense mechanisms. The puffer fish has 3 primary defense mechanisms.

The first defense mechanism is the fish puffs up (thus the name puffer fish). By puffing up, the fish makes itself to be bigger than it really is. When we as humans get hurt we puff ourselves up so that we seem to be bigger than we really are. We puff up to show that despite the fact that we are afraid on the inside everything is alright on the outside.

The second defense mechanism of the puffer fish is spikes that come out of its body. This mechanism tends to run predators off when they get too close. How many times have we run people off and away from us because we believe if they get too close they will hurt us? We even chase away people who may be trying to help us because of our fear of their being too close. Because of this fear, we keep people at arm's length and some we keep away with a ten foot pole.

The third defense mechanism of the puffer fish is that if nothing else works it will emit poison out of its mouth. Well, the Bible says out of our mouths come poison (Romans 3:13). How many times have we said something we later regretted? Why did we say it? Because we were hurt either by something that happened or by something that was said. And in all actuality, this mechanism of defense is really a mechanism of offense. Because we have been hurt so much, instead of being on the receiving end we go on the offensive never to be hurt again. This is what the puffer fish does. This is what I did. This is what humans do, and if you'll be honest, this is what you do.

If someone can scare you off with this, they feel protected even though they are hurting more. If you run off, they think, *you didn't love me anyway.* If you do not run off, but stay there, not forcing your way into their lives but just letting them know they have someone in their corner, they will begin to open up to you. If you willingly put up with someone's worst, they, in turn, will willingly give you their best. Read the following poem and understand what it is saying.

Masking It

Like a thunder storm unleashed in a desert dry,
So do these tears that flood from my heart's eye.
Though invisible, there is a heavy flow,
And unless I told, you'd never know.
You see my courage and not my fear,
But only if there was a window, you'd see clear.
I hurt more than I'll ever tell,
That's the reason for the hard coat shell.
You knock and knock but can't get in,
All because I've got you padlocked, my friend.
If you get too close, it looks like I'll attack,
My bark is ferocious, but I ain't all that.
I pretend, just to keep you away,
Hoping that at a distance you'll stay.
Giving myself time so that my hurt would heal,
Allowing my delicate heart to anneal.
You see my courage and not my fear,
But only if there was a window, you'd see clear.
I hurt more than I'll ever tell,
That's the reason for the hard coat shell.
Though I chase you out, you must find a way in,
So that the process of atonement can begin.
You need me just like I need you.
Now that you know, what are you going to do?

Masking It

There is no amount of anger love cannot conquer. The question is *how much love do you want to give?* I remember my little cousin was over my house and he got mad at me because I would not let him play the piano. You should have seen him, with that little pout on his face, arms crossed, and head down. His cheeks popped out like one of those puffer fish. He even turned his back on me.

Now when I turned my back, as a little child, to an adult, I got whopped upside the head. I almost got mad at him until God helped me to understand he was masking his disappointment by pretending to be mad. So I went over to him and said, *"What? Are you mad at me?"*

He shrugged his head, *yes.*

"Are you still going to play with me?"

He shook his head, *no.*

I told him, "Yes you are."

He shook his head, *no I'm not.*

I said, "Yes you are."

He shook his head, *no I'm not.*

I said, *"Yes you are,"* and I began to tickle him until he smiled, which happened immediately when I started.

He yelled, *"Stop!"* at the top of his two-year-old lungs.

I continued to tickle him, saying, "Oh, I thought you weren't going to talk. Are you talking to me now?"

"Yes," he muttered out in laughter.

"Are you going to play with me," I asked, still tickling him.

"Yes."

After I stopped, he tried to pretend as if he was still mad at me but to no avail. He could not frown straight without laughing. I totally ruined his front. I said to him, *"Quit acting as if you are mad at me. Turn around and give me a hug."* Guess what he did? You guessed it. He wrapped his arms around my neck, squeezed real hard, and he even said, *"I'm sorry."*

God is the same way. Like we already read, God loved us first. He put up with our issues and our locking Him out when we did not trust Him and refuse to let Him in, yet He has always been with us. (Hebrews 13:5). Why? Because we are His children. *(We may think we are adults but we are not. We are children: it is just that some of us have grown up to be older children).*

Sometimes, we just want someone to listen to our hurt and pain, allowing us to be real. Our tensions and angers needs to be released, but sometimes it seems as if no one wants to help us with our issues. But God is always there. In the still of the atmosphere, He sends a cool breeze our way so that we will feel His gentle touch as our body experiences goose bumps. He causes the sun to shine time after time in hopes of creating a brighter day for us. He loves us and He is waiting for us to let Him in. He wants to provide for us the very best life has to offer. He is ever merciful, ever loving, ever caring. He wants to be our *all and all*, if we let Him.

You see, with God, you do not have to mask anything because He sees everything. You could not hide it from Him even if you gave it your best. He saw when you got hurt and He sees how it is affecting you now. Most importantly, He knows how to fix it and wants to, if you let Him.

With God, you can be real and not have to worry about someone taking advantage of your weakness. *The great thing about God is that when you give Him your weakness, He gives you His strength* (2 Corinthians 12:9). However, even though God is there for us, He has also placed other people in our lives so we can have fellowship in this world. They are termed family and friends. The great thing about God is that when you accept Jesus as your Lord and Savior, you are automatically entered into the greatest family in the world.

Now many people have left the body of Christ because people in the church are the very ones that have offended them. Why? Because they see being hurt by the church in the same manner as being hurt by someone in their own family. Let me tell you my friend that Jesus spoke of the woes to those who would bring offense.

Luke 17:1, 2, states: *"Then said he unto the disciples, it is impossible but that offences will come: but woe unto him, through whom they come! It were better for him that a millstone were hanged about his neck, and he cast into the sea, than that he should offend one of these little ones."*

Why? Because He knew we represent Him to others, and when we, as members of the body of Christ, hurt each other, we in turn hurt Christ. Jesus also gave us a method by which we should atone with each other. He calls it communication (Matthew 18:15-20). However, this rarely happens in the church or in our families. So we hurt. And we mask it.

We live in a world of a hurting generation. This generation transcends age brackets: extending from our children who do not have good relationships with their parents now, to the parents, who live in regret of never having had a great relationship with their parents. This hurt, in some way, has helped to mold our viewpoint on life, which may or may not be correct. *Some of us have learned to deal with it; nevertheless, we hurt. Others just mask it.*

The Good Fight

Life's throwing the 1-2 jab
The enemy gets close enough for the back stab.
Cuts and bruises are common place
Sometimes droplets of blood stream down my face.
The pressures of life have got me on bended knee
Targeted for destruction by the enemy.
Jesus he knows and Paul he knew
His attacks on my life only mean he's scared of me too.

Day by day he comes to pick a fight
Huffing and puffing with all his might
Doing his best to blow my house down
Not understanding my foundation is sound.
Sometimes I get rocked, at times I feel a shake
I'm in constant remembrance that my life is at stake.
Yet while down on my knees and a prayer on my tongue
The enemy thinks it's over but really it's just begun.

As I receive God's grace to make it through
You'd best believe I'll remember every blow received from you.
Once upon a time you could hurt me,
Now you're just an aggravating gnat
I've been taking it for too long, now it's time to fight back.
I now have power to tread upon the serpents and scorpions of life
And in a blink of an eye this fight has become a good fight.

Now when you attack I laugh at the best you can do
All I wanna know is whatcha gonna do
when I come for you.
For every time you cause my face to end up in the dirt
For every time I've cried, for every time I've hurt,
For every time you caused me to loose my
heart's desire
For every time you made me walk through the fire,
For every time that I cried, screamed or
made a harsh sound
I dare not give you the pleasure of saying
you took me down.

I will to make it through faith and determination
I overcome failure through patience and
preservation.
You said I couldn't because I was just a man
I say I will, because of Christ I can.
You piled me with burdens saying I couldn't overcome
But I am more than a conqueror because of the blood
of the Son.
No weapon formed against me shall last
because all my burdens upon the Lord I cast.
I can! I shall! I must!!!

Just to prove you out to be the liar you are.
I Will Not Be Defeated!

CHAPTER 6

Learning to Live in Power

Made in the Image of God

The first thing I had to understand was when God recreated me spiritually, I was re-created in the original image of man (Genesis 1:26–28). When God originally made man, He intended him to fulfill the following five elements, which are: 1) be fruitful, 2) multiply, 3) replenish the earth, 4) subdue it, and 5) have dominion over all other creatures. God did not just place man here on Earth to do whatever he feels like. No, God give man a purpose, a predestined path for him to walk in.

However, many of us do not live out our purpose because we live a life of fear. We have been hurt so many times and the pain has been lingering for so long, that we never dare to move out of our comfort zone. Trials and tribulations do not come our way because God is trying to teach us something, but because the Devil does not want us to fulfill God's plan for our lives. Because this is his plan, his greatest attack is on the family.

By him attacking the families and causing our families to become broken, he can effectively disrupt the development of the spirits of the children in our families, who are the lifeline of the world. His plan is to thwart the edifying of our faith in the authority God has given us. If he can stop our development as children, when we become adults we will not walk in the power we should. Furthermore, we will not be able to teach our children how to walk and follow after God. This is where we have missed it with our families.

In Matthew 13:3-8, Jesus teaches about the parable of the sower. There are four types of ground the sower planted seed in. The first type of ground is *"by the way side"* mentality. These are people who do not have any interest whatsoever in the Word, but trust in their own ability, because they do not understand some things in the Word. Instead of receiving wisdom and revelation from God, they try to think things out.

The second type of ground is *"stony ground"*. These people hear the Word and want to act on it. However, these people are nearsighted and as a result, Satan brings trials and tribulations in their line of sight. Because they cannot see the promise or the *end* result, they give up and become offended. Offense will cause one's heart to become stony. When this occurs, their hearts are so hard they will not receive anything from anyone.

The third type is the *"thorny ground"*. These people want the promises of the Bible but will not do what it takes to get them. For example, they want prosperity but they feel if they pay tithes they will not have enough money to make it. They go through life always trying to get out from under the debt they incur; thereby, being choked by the thorns of life.

Then there is the fourth type of ground, which is deemed *"good ground"*. This kind of person not only hears the Word, but they also have understanding of the Word. They take the understanding they have and act on it, which causes them to be fruitful. Most Christians fit into categories two and three, but for the purposes of gaining understanding, God only wants me to deal with category two, which is stony ground.

Many people have left the Church and abandoned Christianity because of being offended. (They have experienced some event that traumatically affected their lives. They believed God would intervene on their behalf, but their petition for some reason was not answered). They became offended at God because they did not get the response they were looking for, and their hearts turned stony towards His Word.

This is what has happened to many of the people (children) even though they may have attended church every Sunday. One day they determine the Church has no real power to address issues in the community so they decide to leave with a false hope of trying to find something that can. We hear about the God of the Bible, but we do not see the God of the Bible in our lives. So what do we do? We go about our lives masking the fear we are truly living in.

I remember saying to myself one time, "Why pray? Nothing is going to change. My circumstances are the way they are and I will just have to do the best I can."

Because of this mentality there were certain things I did not do because I did not try. Why? I was living in fear; therefore, I did not believe. However, God wanted to get me to understand I was not made to be subject to my circumstances, but they were made to be subject to me. This is true because I am made in His image, and because of that truth, there are five elements that should be apparent in my life. For our purposes, we will only look at elements four and five, which are subdue and have dominion.

Boxed in a Stereotype

Growing up without a natural father around to help develop my character and confidence, the world placed me in a box and said I would fit a certain kind of stereotype. Read the following news article by Maggie Gallagher for the Wall Street Journal on December 1, 1998:

Boys Without Fathers More Prone to Crime

Criminologists have long suspected the absence of a father in the home is an important factor in leading boys into violence and crime. But since there are so many other variables involved such as the mother's education, race, income, unemployment rates and even cognitive ability, it has been impossible to say with any certainty how family structure alone figures in the equation. Now, Cynthia Harper of the University of California and Sara McLanahan of Princeton University have utilized a large national database, the National Longitudinal Survey of Youth, to control for those variables and isolate the family structure question. Among their findings:

- Boys raised outside of intact marriages are, on average, more than twice as likely as other boys to wind up in jail, with each year spent without a dad increasing the odds of future incarceration by 5 percent.
- A child born to an unwed mother is about 2.5 times more likely to end up in prison, while one whose parents split during his teen years was about 1.5 times more likely to be imprisoned.
- Boys living in stepparent families were almost 3 times as likely to face incarceration.
- While living in poverty made it more likely a boy would go to jail, *family structure was more important than income.*
- Teenage boys living with just their single fathers were no more likely to commit crimes than boys coming from intact families. But boys living with remarried fathers faced rates of future incarceration as high as or higher than boys living with remarried mothers.[1]

Because my father left when I was age 5, society said I had a 65% chance of being incarcerated by age 18, but God said, *"Not so."* Look at these statistics and you will see what my life was up against. The following is a sample of what other sources have had to say about the risks faced by fatherless children:

- 63% of youth suicides are from fatherless homes (Source: U.S. D.H.H.S., Bureau of the Census)
- 85% of all children that exhibit behavioral disorders come from fatherless homes (Source: Center for Disease Control)
- 80% of rapists motivated with displaced anger come from fatherless homes (Source: Criminal Justice & Behavior, Vol. 14, p. 403-26, 1978).
- 71% of all high school dropouts come from fatherless homes (Source: National Principals Association Report on the State of High Schools).
- 70% of juveniles in state operated institutions come from fatherless homes (Source: U.S. Dept. of Justice, Special Report, Sept 1988)
- 85% of all youths sitting in prisons grew up in a fatherless home (Source: Fulton Co. Georgia jail populations, Texas Dept. of Corrections 1992) [2]

I want you to note *85% of all children that exhibit behavioral disorders come from fatherless homes.* From the last chapter we understand the behavior exhibited is due to them masking their fears and hurts from society. This was the stereotype I had to fight against in my own life. Not having a father in a child's life will produce a life of fear.

We read in the first article a boy that lives with a single father as his parent is more likely to image the behavior of those who have their families intact. This is true because a father teaches survival. If a father is not there to teach survival then the child will grow up having to learn survival on his own without a guide.

A father is also a protector. Without someone there to protect us, we feel vulnerable to the world; therefore, we become as the puffer fish, inflating our egos, attitudes, and anger towards all that would cross our paths. It is a self-defense mechanism. When met with resistance, we puff up. When asked to submit, we puff up. And if you get too close, you will get stuck by the spikes that extend out of us.

Just like the puffer fish, when we feel you have placed us in a dire position, we will cause poison to come out of us. The sad thing is that we puff up so much it becomes a lifestyle. Even though that lifestyle is filled with anger and rage, the truth of the matter is we are scared because there is no one there to teach us how to become the men we are supposed to be.

This was the way my life began. There were times when the anger inside of me was so great and full of pressure I thought my heart would burst. Because I did not know what was going on, I would release this pressure in the first manifestation that would come to mind. Sometimes it would come out as me breaking things. Other times it would come out as me hitting people.

While in middle school (grades 6th through 8th), I engaged in over twenty fights. That is almost seven fights per year. A school year is only nine months, which means I got into a fight almost every month of the school year. It was only the favor of God as to why I did not get suspended. The most I ever received was detention, and sometimes I did not get anything. All I knew was I did not want to live in fear any longer, and I was not.

No More Spirit of Fear

In learning to be a son of God, He taught me I was not given a spirit of fear. It is not in my character (2 Timothy 1:7). When I received God as my heavenly Father, He gave me His Spirit and nowhere included in His Spirit is found the element of fear. Yet there was fear found in me. You see, even though I am a son of God I still have to develop His character (fruit of the Spirit) within.

Not only that, but I have to gain confidence in who I am. I have to understand I was given a Spirit of power, authority, love, self-appreciation, and a sound and unwavering mind. By operating in these aspects of the Spirit of God, I become confident in Him and who He made me to be.

I am now able to go through life without fearing failure. Now, I am not acting in my power and authority, but in His power and His authority, which is given to me to deal with situations. The love and appreciation I have does not come from me, but from Him, and His love is given to me to deal with people. My ability to have a sound and unwavering mind does not come from the fact that I have no worries, but from the fact that I trust in Him, and my trusting in Him gives me stability. When I draw strength from His Spirit, I have no need to live in fear.

The Spirit of Power

In Luke 10:19, Jesus states that we can operate in two categories of power. The first word power is translated from the Greek word *exousia, which means the power of rule or government (the power of him whose will and commands must be submitted to by others and obeyed)*. The terms serpents and scorpions refer to things that may come in your life to poison it. Encounters with these species usually brings about fear with most people and pain if one has been struck by them.

Likewise, in life, most people fear going through trials and tribulations, and by and large, experience agony while going through them. However, according to this verse, God has given unto me the authority to bring under subjection everything wrong in my life. I no longer have to fear when I see something coming my way that may come up against me.

This verse is not talking about treading upon real snakes and scorpion, but situations brought to us by the Devil and his demons. The situations this verse is talking about are trials, tribulations, persecutions, distresses, and temptations. From these things, I do not have to run, nor will I. I have been given the ability by God to meet these issues head on. I have the authority to regulate how I respond to situations in life.

The second word translated power comes from the Greek word *dunamis*, which means inherent power, power residing in a thing by virtue of its nature, or which a person or thing exerts and puts forth. Not only do I have authority over any trial that may be brought my way, but I also have authority over the one who brings it my way, who is ultimately Satan.

No weapon, even though it may be dynamic in its working, that is formed against me can become a success, and every one that comes against me (wrongfully) I have the ability to condemn (Isaiah 54:17). This is my heritage, my right, and I have the authority to do so. This is a part of my right standing with God. However, I want you to note the weapon will only fail if I stand up to it and condemn it.

Too many times we become victims of situations because we do not say anything. We keep our mouths shut and do nothing to confront the situation. We take upon ourselves this *"I am a victim"* mentality and believe we are subject to our fate when the opposite is true. I am not subject to my fate. My fate is subject to me because I have been given authority to take control of my destiny. I am no longer a victim.

My life is not subject to the stereotypes and labels society tries to pigeonhole me into. No, I tell society I am the exception to the rule. I speak to my destiny and I overcome. (*However, with authority comes responsibility. God has shown me in my life, many of the issues I came up against were because I did not take responsibility for my actions. I messed up and I was reaping the consequences*).

I never have to be a victim in my life ever again. I will not be a victim to situations that life brings my way. I will not be a victim to persecutions brought on me by other people. I will not even be a victim to circumstances in my life due to decisions that I have made. I am created to be a dominator. All problems I encounter I place under my feet; therefore, I tread upon all circumstances that may try to magnify themselves in my life.

I remember I used to walk with my head hung down and my shoulders slouched over; but when God showed me who He made me to be, a dominator, I began to walk with my shoulders squared and my chin up.

I am created to be an overcomer (I John 4:4). I am a child of God and His Spirit lives in me. I have the ability to deal with any trial and tribulation this world can place before me because greater is the power that resides within me and the fortress surrounding me than any weapon that might be brought against me.

I am created to be more than a conqueror. There is no condemnation that can be brought my way if *(and only if)* I walk in the fruit of the Spirit of God (Romans 8:1). God has justified me and if God says I am righteous, who's word is so great it can contradict that of my Lord. This confidence I now have not because of who I am or because of the power I have, but only because of the love of God.

The Spirit of Love (1 John 4:18)

When a person lives a life filled with fear, their life is filled with anxiety and worry. They experience restless nights and are afraid of how their circumstances may affect them. They go through torment of the mind. Why? They do not know how much God loves them. Even today, I am still learning about the love of God. If God is on my side, what can men, circumstances, or trials do to me? According to the verse, *perfect love* casts out fear. For this cause, I have no need to be afraid. However, I want you to notice something about this love. It is a balance to power. Many people acquire power and they do not have love. When this happens, abuse occurs. When abuse of power is prevalent, it leads to strife and seditions. Strife and sedition leads to confusion and every manner of evil work (James 3:16). The power you are given causes you to take authority over the situation; however, God expects us to still walk in love towards the one(s) who may be participating in causing us tribulation. In our love walk, we are supposed to overcome anything that is done to us through love (Romans 12:17-21).

Please realize it does not take much to allow your flesh to have a temper tantrum, but it takes real power to be able to subdue your own flesh. Yeah, God gives you dominion and you have been endued with power to place all things under your feet; however, God never intended for us to dominate each other and He never intended for us to place someone else under our feet. The authority God has given us is over the situations and attacks the enemy brings against our lives.

When it comes to people, God expects us to treat people like we would like to be treated. This is a *hard saying*. But your ability to do this speaks to your faith and love toward God. Furthermore, God says He is going to take vengeance on those who do not do right by you. When you know God loves you, you will believe He is going to shield you.

They may not get what they deserve right away, and in fact, it may be years before anything happens, but that is only because God is merciful. He is giving them time to get it right before He steps in. The problem is our flesh wants to see them suffer and that is not godly. God's plan is for us to be able to work things out with each other as stated in Matthew 18:15–19. However, there are some people that are just impossible to deal with.

That is why God says to live in peace with all men, *as much as you possibly can.* When you have done all, and that person just will not change their ways, you are no longer obligated to try to deal with that person. This does not mean now you can take vengeance into your hands. It just means now you have the right to stand still and see the salvation of the Lord. However, you cannot stand until you have done all (Ephesians 6:13).

As stated earlier, as sons of God we have been given power (authority) over the situation, not over the person. Therefore, we must exercise wisdom in dealing with the person while exercising authority in dealing with the situation. Too many times we try to exercise authority over the person causing the situation to really get out of hand. In most cases, one person tries to force what they think on the other person. In doing this, what you are saying is *I take authority over your thoughts and opinions and I subject what you are thinking to what I say.* This is wrongly motivated, selfish, and it is the sin of witchcraft. God gave you power; however, the power He gave you is to be exercised over your flesh.

You cannot control people (that is the sin of witchcraft), but you can control yourself. In order to properly handle conflicts with people we need to put on the whole armor of God.

Most people think when you put on the whole armor of God you are to then just stand there waiting on God to fight your battles. What it really means is, *continue to do what you've been doing, to stay firmly established.* In the context of Ephesians 6, Paul is writing to the saints about how to deal with other people. As a child of God, you must understand your problem is not with that person but with Satan. You must also understand Satan wants to cause division between people, especially in our families.

In dealing with people, you must put on the whole armor of God. The armor consists of the following elements: truth, righteousness, peace, faith, salvation, the Word of God, and prayer. *(Note: We do not usually see prayer as part of the armor because it was not symbolized as anything but this is a powerful weapon to utilize).* This is what God means when He tells us to put on the whole armor of God. These pieces of armor are characteristics God wishes us to wear every day.

When you are standing in the whole armor of God, the enemy will not have a chance against you. Trust me; it will take the love of God operating in you to do this. If we will be honest with ourselves, we love to be right and we love to win. Having authority over other people makes us feel powerful. However, true power is the ability to bring your own flesh under the subjection of your will. When you accept Jesus into your life, you gain the power to operate in this armor.

To love someone that is seemingly unlovable is the most powerful thing you could ever do. Some people act undesirably, but when you are operating in the power of God's might through His Spirit of Love, it can be done. Paul ran into a problem with someone who became as a thorn in his side. This person buffeted him (attacked him through verbal abuse) for three years. Paul was able to find strength to forbear this person because he operated in the power of God in order to do so (2 Corinthians 12:9).

When somebody attacks you and you gather strength from God not to retaliate; that is living in power. If everyone retaliates when they are attacked, the world would be in a worse condition than it currently is. Normally when we retaliate, we try to dominate the other person. However, living in power is not about dominating people. Living in power is about having the ability to move forward despite what other people are doing to you.

In life, God places people in our lives to show us His love by helping us, so we do have to deal with people; however, God never intended for our lives to be dependent upon others. There is interdependence between people but *our dependence should be established in God.* I made a decision early in life I would be successful even if I had to do it by myself. Thank God, I was never by myself. I had the help of the Father leading and guiding me, as a good father should. Why? Because He loves me, and He loves you too.

The Spirit of a Sound Mind (Philippians 4:7)

If you are going to learn to live in power, you will have to learn *not to be moved* by circumstances and people. This is a lesson I learned all too well. In order to live in power, you must have stability. If you do not have stability you will be continually uprooted and tossed by the winds and waves of life (James 1:6–8).

As a son of God, I am developing into a man of God. Now a man of God is not measured by age, but is measured by stability in Him. In other words, my mind is settled. Once I know what my Father's position is, I know what my position is. I become rooted and grounded in Him. Society says I am supposed to fail, but God said I am an overcomer. My mind is settled. Statistics say I will succumb to crime, drugs, behavioral problems, and abuse, but God said I would conquer these things. My mind is settled. My background places me in a stereotype that says I will be defeated in life, but God said no weapon formed against me shall prosper. My mind is settled.

God had to constantly remind me what His thoughts concerning me were. I had to get to the point where I believed what God said about me over what society, statistics, my background, and other individuals may have said. This is my confidence that God loves me and because He loves me, my self-esteem is in Him. I am not some big shot nor did I come from a family that has had it made, but I gave my life to a God that said He would uphold me in my weakness. I am not who I am because of where I come from. I am who I am because of what God is making me to be. Like Paul, I know whose I am and whom I serve (Acts 27:23).

It matters not what I have done in the past, nor yet where I have been; but what matters is who I will allow God to make me to be. My success is a settled issue because I have placed my trust in God. He is the only sure thing because He changes not (Malachi 3:6) and His Word is forever settled in Heaven (Psalms 119:89). If I place my confidence in man, I have no sure foundation. Man changes his ways and his mind. If I place my confidence in things, I have no sure foundation. Things come and go. They lose value and appeal. When I place my confidence in Him, I know what the outcome is going to be.

Because God is my rock, that means I can stand on a sure foundation (Psalms 18:2). This means He will bring stability to my life. I am building my life upon a solid foundation and Jesus Christ is the chief cornerstone. Because God is my fortress, that means I *shall* be protected from the snares of the enemy. I may be attacked but as long as I stay within the fortress, it shall not harm me. Because God is my deliverer, when I find myself in situations and circumstances too great for me to handle, I know He will come to my rescue. As a Father, He has given me His guarantee.

Because God is my buckler, when it seems the pressures of life are causing me to fall apart, I *rest assured* God will hold my life together. When it feels like I am going to lose it, I find myself in Him. God is the horn of my salvation. In times of distress, I call upon my God and He hears me and answers my cry. Because God is my high tower, when negativity and pessimism try to pull me down, He elevates my mind to a higher platform. He takes me to a place where I can overlook my problems and clearly see into the distance the beauty of the land He has promised me. All of this is because I trust Him. This is my confidence that God always has, always is, and always will be there for me. He is my stability, and because God is no respecter of persons, He will do the same for you.

True Power

There is a quote I saw one time that simply says, *You can tell how big a person is by what it takes to discourage them.* In other words, what does it take to move you? For some people, all you have to do is step on the corns of their feet and they will curse you. For others, they can lose everything and still have a positive outlook because they know with God on their side they still win. Their mentality is: *the bigger the obstacle, the greater the triumph.*

In my case, I had to overcome being discouraged about not having a father. However, I could not let it be my excuse for not succeeding. Furthermore, God is my Father and He has given me the ability to deal with any and every situation the enemy has to bring. I operate in His power to successfully deal with situations. I operate in His love to successfully deal with people. I operate in a sound mind, having stability in Him, which causes me not to be moved by either. For God has not given me a spirit of fear, but of power, and of love, and of a sound mind.

Endnotes

1 Maggie Gallagher (Institute for American Values), "Fatherless Boys Grow Up Into Dangerous Men," Wall Street Journal, 1 December. 1998.
2 "Fatherless Boys at Risk." Fathering Magazine. November, 2002. 11 November, 2002. <http://www.fathermag.com/809/sanfrancisco.shtml>

Transparent

Make me transparent, oh God,
See through me so I might be known,
Examine my inner most being,
Try my thoughts and my ways
that they might be proved.

Thou seest my ingoing and my going forth,
My path is known by Thee,
Ordained steps do I take,
a road not crooked but straight,
Yearning so earnestly to fulfill my fate.

Open the door of my life,
Make known my hidings; no secrets here,
Door by door, room by room, come see how I live,
Yes, let us sup together, me and You.

And after You have assessed my dwellings,
Correct me, completely straighten my path,
Show me a more perfect way, oh Ancient of Days,
Direct and guide me in the way of Thy righteousness.

I am become transparent
Open my ears that I might hear,
Open my eyes that I might see,
Open my mind that I might understand,
Open my heart that I might love.

I am become transparent so that You may know me.

Forgiveness

Father, let me look through your eyes to see
Your children as you created them to be.
Too many times I focus on their imperfection,
Not seeing that they are all your election.
Let me see so that I might know
And appreciate all the colors of your bow.

Let me not see their sins,
But let me know their hearts as friends.
May our spirits dance together in peace,
May we live our lives in harmony and ease.

And may they see me as do you,
So we may know each other as the Spirit says to.
I forgive that I would be forgiven divine,
I forget never again to remember the time.
Let us fitly join together in the Body of You,
So we may dwell together as the Spirit says to.

In Need of Healing

Sometimes my spirit cries,
Even though the tears never make it to my eyes,
Going around wearing a disguise,
I say everything's all right, but I'm speaking lies.

I have the power to control my hurt,
But only God can heal,
I force myself to mask the pain;
However, I long to be real.

I speak forgiveness from the heart,
I have let the situation go,
But why is the pain still there,
The answer I do not know.

Lord, forgive me for lying
About what I thought I gave to you,
You know that my heart is sincere
And that I don't know what to do.

With my mouth I say, "Release,"
Yet it is my spirit that holds on,
I say that I can move forward,
Even though the pain isn't gone.

Lord, heal my hurt,
Help me to be more like you,
Help me to nail forgiveness to the Cross,
Just as you did for me too.

I Receive My Healing.

Chapter 7

Living in Love & Forgiveness

Dealing with the Past

Romans 12:21 states: *Be not overcome of evil, but overcome evil with good.*

Some of the greatest obstacles in our lives that keep us from moving forward into the future are our past hurts. Like myself, many people grew up resenting their fathers because they were not there for them. Or maybe their fathers were there, but they was not much of a father to them at all. This brings forth hurt and resentment, and after a period of time bitterness sets in. This root of bitterness springs forth from the heart and it begins to consume that person from the inside out. If we do not live in love and forgiveness, bitterness will overcome us and we will live defeated lives.

We see people all the time who have not made anything of their lives, and when you speak with them about it, they tell you the reason why they are not making it in life is because of this or that. As a matter of fact, there are religions based upon the hatred of one group of people and some see them as the reason why they have not been able to make it. The truth of the matter is if you do not make it in this life, *it is not because of anyone but you.*

We cannot go through life blaming other people for what is, or what is not happening in our lives. Yes, God *has* placed people in our lives to help us through, but if the person is not doing right, God is not going to say, *"Oh well, that was the only person I had to help you and since they are not going to do what you want them to do, you just have to accept being a failure."* God loves you so much He is going to make sure you are not left alone. To God, people are vessels through which He can flow into the lives of others; however, as people, we have to be willing vessels to allow God to do so.

As willing vessels, we become open to God and His will. Sometimes God will place someone in our lives to help us through a trying situation. Friends are people God uses to show us His love. However, at the same time God wants to show His love through us into the lives of other people. He cannot do that if we are filled with bitterness and resentment in our hearts. As a man is in his heart, so is he. (Proverbs 23:7)

Being filled with bitterness and resentment hinders the flow of God into your life. We already learned God wants the fruit of His Spirit to operate in our lives, and three of the fruit are to flow from God into us and then into others. These three are love, joy, and peace. The opposite of these three are hatred, bitterness, and confusion. So if we are filled with bitterness, then the fruit of joy cannot operate in our lives.

Many times when we become filled with bitterness and resentment, we either externalize it or we internalize it. When we externalize it, we exhibit mood swings, temper tantrums, etc. We push people away by the things we do and very few people will tolerate us or our actions. When we internalize it, we tend to go into seclusion and we never really deal with the problem. We close people out by not letting them into our lives: we block them out and very few people will actually take the time to find a way in. Trust me, I understand what it means to be hurt by someone you respect and love. I have been there with my father. He was supposed to be there for me and when he was not, I felt abandoned and vulnerable. *Who was going to lead me? Who was going to teach me to be a man? Who would call me son? Who would I have such a relationship with?* Today, I am still in search of a father.

However, I cannot put life on pause and wait for someone to come along and say, *"I want to help you out."* God may tell someone to help me but they have to be willing to do it (remember, a person must be a willing vessel). If they are not willing then guess what, life goes on. You cannot build your life being dependent upon people. People will let you down and if you have based your entire future upon that person, you will be thoroughly devastated when they do.

Too many times we want people to come and hold us up when we are down. We want to use them as crutches to lean on, especially if we have been wounded in life. A person is under no obligation to do so; however, God is. God gave me a promise He would be there for me even when no one else would be. Why would He care so much? Because He is my Father, and just as a natural father should be there to make sure His son is successful, my heavenly Father is watching over my every step to make sure I do not slip (Psalm 18:36). He loves me, and guess what: He loves you just as much.

Love and Forgiveness

Regardless of how I may have been treated in the past, as a child of God, I have to walk in love and forgiveness. I understand this is easier said than done, but the fact of the matter is *it can be done*. The reason why many cannot do it is because they do not know how. If I took a survey of how many people walked in the fruit of the Spirit (based upon what we learned in an earlier chapter), a great deal of people would not do so well.

I know it is a struggle. It is so easy just to react to how we feel; however, even when we react to how we feel the pain inside does not go away. In most cases, what we end up doing is hurting someone else. And every time we feel the pain, we react and hurt someone else. This cycle goes on and on until we habitually victimize others so we will not feel as if we are victims, thereby, deceiving ourselves because we feel empowered. However, transferring this pain to someone else is really just our sharing it, because the pain is still there.

The only way to truly deal with hurt and sorrow is to operate in love and forgiveness. This is a process; something you have to do on a continual basis. You have to deal with your flesh everyday because it wants to release and transfer the pain. Your flesh says to take revenge, but the Spirit of God, the Holy Ghost, wants to constrain you. Our soul agrees with our flesh because we have been taught all our lives we should not take anything negative or derogatory from anyone, lest we are looked upon as being soft. After all, we live in a cold world, right?

When you think about how gangs operate, one person offends another and the friends of the two opponents get involved. You kill my boy and I will kill yours. This scenario goes back and forth as both sides try to release and transfer their pain. This pain is spread to others as innocent victims die, making the problem worse. Where does it stop? The only way for the violence to stop is for someone to start living in forgiveness. The only way to truly forgive is to have the love of God inside of you to constrain you from reacting.

In my case, I was bitter toward my father; however, my father was not around so I could not express my bitterness toward him. Therefore, I took it out on my mother and grandparents and others who would dare challenge me. I would release and transfer this pain to people who had nothing to do with my father leaving. In essence, because I had unforgivness toward my father, I made others feel my pain through rebellion, improper behavior, and other violent outlets.

Forgiveness. Not operating in forgiveness can clog you up spiritually and mentally. When you do not forgive someone, essentially you are saying I do not want to move forward in life until that person comes and repays me for the hurt and pain they caused me, which may or may not happen. A person who has hurt you may or may not come to you and apologize. Even if they did, there is no guarantee their apology would ease your pain.

Spiritually. Unforgiveness clogs you spiritually because it harbors hatred. We know according to 1 John 4:8, *God is Love*. Because we are vessels through which God flows, we must be open to what flows out of Him, and one of the most important that flows out of Him is love. If we harbor hatred, we cannot accept love, which means we cannot accept God. Operating in unforgiveness is like putting a lid on a cup so no fluid can be poured in. And if God cannot pour himself into your life, then He cannot pour His blessings into your life either. There is a direct correlation between forgiving and having your prayers answered.

In Matthew 5:23, 24, Jesus tells us before we come to God with our offering, which is a form of worshipping and showing Him our love, we should first go to our brother and clear up any offenses. God is just as interested in being able to bless someone through you, as a vessel, as He is in you blessing Him. God owns everything, so when we give Him something it belongs to Him anyway. However, when we allow God to flow through us in forgiveness towards all men, that is one of the greatest forms of worship we can give unto Him. When worshipping God by allowing His character to be seen through you becomes your lifestyle, then God will begin to honor your prayers. When God sees you will deny your flesh to obey Him, He sees that as an even greater sacrifice than any amount of money you could give. Remember, your blessing from God is only dependent upon your obedience, which means if God is not seemingly answering your prayers you need to take a good look in the mirror to see why.

He also is making a direct correlation between forgiving and being forgiven. Everyone makes mistakes and deserves to be forgiven. I am not saying we should subject ourselves to that person, *especially if they have not done anything to prove they have changed.* Sometimes when someone hurts us the relationship is never the same. This is a truth we must acknowledge; however, that does not mean that we have to hold it against them for the rest of their lives. God does not hold sin against us for the rest of our lives and neither should we.

In my case, I learned to forgive my father by the age of sixteen. However, the relationship we had from then on was nowhere near the relationship we had when I was age five. There was nothing that he could have done to make up for not being there. He was still my dad, but not my father. The term father denotes a relationship with someone upon whom you can lean and go to for protection, guidance, and comfort, which we do not have in our relationship.

We are more like friends, not that I still have resentment towards him, but it is hard to view him as my father. Does that mean that I am living in unforgiveness? No. It just means that I could not view him as my father given the previous definition of what a father is. I love my dad with all my heart and he has my full forgiveness, but he chose to abandon his position, not me. Furthermore, my days of being raised are pretty much over.

Please understand when the Bible talks about walking in love, it does not mean everything will be the way it should have been. Walking in love means you are not holding bitterness in your heart towards that person. It does not mean the relationship will be the best of relationships. In fact, some relationships are destroyed beyond repair. The closeness, respect, honor, and emotional feelings may be gone permanently.

There is still much I can learn, but when I look at his life today and see that he is still searching for happiness, I can only learn from his mistakes. As I stated earlier, at the age of five I determined I would make it with or without him. Furthermore, I determined in my heart to surpass him. These comments are not to put my father down, but I had to assume or operate in this mentality in order to succeed. Still, he is forgiven, but the emotional relationship is not there.

I have spent so much time detaching myself from him, so I would not stay hurt, that our relationship seems distant. Not that I do not want a relationship with my dad, it is just not there for right now, but we are working on some things. Guess what? That does not mean I do not love him. There are levels to love and they are determined by the quality of our relationship and our fellowship with one another.

In the case of my relationship with my dad, a trust was destroyed. What we must understand is that a person can forgive someone without trusting that person. A good example of that can be seen in the life of David, the greatest king of Israel [outside of Jesus]. There was a time when he was under attack by King Saul and David never did anything to retaliate. However, David knew when it was time for him to leave, and because there was not any trust between them, he went and lived among the Philistines.

In Psalm 55:12–14, David is writing about Saul, a man whom he considered to be like a father. David loved him, but not at the risk of submitting his life to this man who repeatedly tried to kill him. Where there is no trust, there can be no relationship. Before roles and responsibilities can be set in a relationship, a foundation of trust must be established. There is no way around this. On the other hand, if you are offended, you do have to be open to the person who hurt you, but they must prove themselves trustworthy. God does not expect you to have to be dependent upon someone who has not proven their worth.

Another reason why I learned I must forgive my dad is because if I do not, I may fall into the same temptation he did (Galatians 6:1). We have to be careful that we do not fall into the same scenario the people who offended us did. By not forgiving a person, we allow the same temptation to come into our lives. All this is a part of the spiritual aspect of forgiveness. We do not acknowledge this because we do not see the spiritual side of things, but that does not mean it is not true. The simple fact that a person offended you means they fell into temptation. That does not mean anything at all, because we all fall from time to time, so who are we to look down on other people.

However, I want you to notice something. Many people today who get divorced had parents who got divorced. That bitterness, anger, and unforgiveness, towards their parents falling into that temptation came into their lives also, and caused them to fall as well. Why? Because unforgiveness in that area allows for that same demonic temptation to enter your life. (Selah. Pause and think about that).

Mentally: Unforgiveness causes us to get stuck in the past. Many times, the offense clouds our thinking and all we can think about is how someone hurt us. We become so focused on nursing our hurts we tend to neglect other things in life. Harboring unforgiveness causes us to turn all of our attention inwardly. By doing so, we become self-conscious and bitter towards others (Hebrews 12:14, 15).

One definition for the word defile means corrupt. Many times being offended corrupts our thinking and our judgment. When we are bitter the smallest thing will cause us to erupt. This is defilement. Our minds become clouded with what we are going through and soon the enemy begins to make us think no one understands what we are going through: no one is on our side. Now we are thinking everyone is our enemy. We allow one person to destroy our trust with everyone.

A good example of this can be seen in women who have been hurt by other men and they say, *"All men are dogs."* Not only that, but they spread their defilement to their friends. Why? Because they are bitter and their judgment is defiled.

Their thinking is clouded and when a good man comes their way, they loses him because he does not want to deal with all the issues they have. And instead of looking at themselves, they just reassures themselves that men are dogs.

This can also be applied to the bastard mentality. Growing up without a father causes many children not to trust men in authority. I know it did for me. A woman could ask me to do something or give me a suggestion and I could take it with no problem. A man, on the other hand, could do the same thing and I would not receive it. Why? Women have my trust because of who my mother is to me. Men *did* not have my trust because of who my father was to me (but I have learned to change this). All of this is a mental decision I made and changing how I make decisions is just as simple as having *a change of heart* (Romans 12:2).

Renewing your mind in the area of forgiving someone is a 24-7 activity. You have to constantly live in forgiveness because it is so easy to fall right back into resentment. You may think you are over it one day, but when something goes wrong in your life it is so easy for you to look at someone else to blame, because that is what it is really about. So many people resent others because they feel a persons or persons have destroyed their lives. Many times when we do not receive a desire or dream it is so easy to place the blame elsewhere.

However, in the perfect will of God your blessing is dependent upon you. Now it helps to be in a good church that teaches and preaches the Word of God, but the blessing in your life will be based upon your personal relationship with God. You can be a part of the greatest church in the world, but if you do not make the decision to follow after the Word of God you will not succeed.

This is something I had to make a mental note of. When I learned this, I no longer resented my dad over the fact that he did not teach me how to become a man. I gained a personal relationship with my heavenly Father, and He taught me to be a man, and the first thing He taught me was I can do all things through Christ who is my strength (Philippians 4:13).

My mind was renewed to this, and this is what has caused me to be more than a conqueror.

Love. One of the Greek words for forgiveness is *charizomai*, which means *"to bestow a favor unconditionally."* To favor someone means to show them good will; to prefer one; to treat as special. *Treat special?* Yeah, I was thinking the same thing you are thinking now: *There ain't anything special about this person.* Why would God expect me to give favor to this person? Because forgiveness is an act of love, an act of God.

But God, how can I love this person when I do not even like them? The answer to this question is as simple as knowing the difference between love and like. Like is a feeling while love is an action. You may not be able to yet control how you feel towards someone, but you can control your actions towards them. God wants us to be kindly affectionate towards one another. This is denoting an action, which means it can and should be done out of love. This verse also says *"preferring."* This again denotes an action being done. And before you ever do an action, you first have to make a decision.

As a child of God, you are recreated in the image of His dear Son. You are given the fruit of His Spirit. You have the ability to love because God is love and He lives in you. Is it easy? No! If it were, there would be no need for me to write this book. The more you practice walking in love the more you will be able to control your feelings, but it will not happen overnight.

If you have noticed, I have focused mainly on developing myself. When I become mature I can endure how people treat me and still come out on top. There is a saying *"He who angers you controls you as well."* No one deserves that much power. Therefore, unforgiveness causes you to live under the spirit of bondage, which is of fear. However, God has given us His Spirit, which includes power to overcome the situation, love to forgive the person, and a sound mind to be able to move forward in life.

You see, perfect love casts out fear. A perfect example of this is the life of Joseph. Can you imagine being thrown in a pit by your brothers and left there? Not only was he thrown into a pit but he was also sold to some Ishmaelites that took him to Egypt. Once Joseph arrived in Egypt, he was sold into slavery. However, even as a slave he was determined to be the best possible person he could be. The only way to do this was to live in forgiveness and stay focused on where he was going, not where he had been. You see, unforgiveness will keep you in the past and you will never move forward. If only both blacks and whites would recognize this, America would be a much better place. Racism and segregation would be fully eliminated if both races would operate in love and forgiveness.

Because of Joseph's attitude, God caused him to prosper. Because Joseph operated in forgiveness, he had an excellent spirit, which simply means he did not complain about his current situation. The main reason Joseph did not complain was because he received a dream from God: a dream of greatness and of purpose. By focusing on where he was going he did not give much time to think about where he came from. He also knew if he did not forgive, he would not achieve his dreams of the future, because unforgiveness would have kept him in the past.

Now the Bible does not say how Joseph was affected by what his brothers did to him. All we know is he became second only to Pharaoh in the land of Egypt. In other words, he went from being a slave to being a prince. Joseph allowed love to carry him from the dungeon to the palace. This was despite what happened to him.

Love will cause you to operate above those around you. Love, also known as charity, is not a feeling of passion, but a character trait that entails many qualities, one of which is forgiveness.

According to 1 Corinthians 13:4-8a: *"Charity suffereth long, and is kind; charity envieth not; charity vaunteth not itself, is not puffed up, Doth not behave itself unseemly, seeketh not her own, is not easily provoked, thinketh no evil; Rejoiceth not in iniquity, but rejoiceth in the truth;* **Beareth all things, believeth all things, hopeth all things, endureth all things. Charity never faileth:** . . ."

Most people think forgiveness is pretending something never happened. That is not forgiveness; that is justification. Justification is the ability to wipe a record clean, just as if it never happened. Only God can justify, because only He has the ability to blot out a transgression; however, we cannot. Even if we could, the Devil would continuously bring it back to our mind. Therefore, God only asks us to forgive.

When you forgive someone you make a conscious decision to put up with their flaws and faults. Not only that, but you treat them with kindness despite how they treat you. You are not plotting on how you can get revenge. You control yourself to patiently bear whatsoever they may dish out. You keep believing one day their actions will not stir your emotions. You keep hoping they will begin to act in love towards you the way you act in love towards them. When you forgive you endure the situation until the pain no longer hurts.

Forgiveness ***does not happen overnight.*** It does happen step by step. There will be times when you will cry. There will be times when you will just want to give up. There will even be times when you cannot see the dream you so desperately desire, because your mind is clouded with thoughts of what that person did or did not do. Trust me, I have been there. However, I have learned everyday I feel like giving up I just remind myself of my dreams. By constantly keeping them before me, I stay focused on my future, that which is important. See (Psalm 27:13, 14.)

Joseph knew the hurt he endured was but for a season. Most people faint because they do not see the blessing they are going to receive because of their willingness to forgive. However, as the Psalmist says, *"wait on the LORD."*

As stated before, forgiveness is a process. Joseph still had a little resentment in his heart towards his brothers, and we see that in Genesis 42-44. In these chapters, Joseph's heart was to place fear and torment in the lives of his brothers for what they did; however, we see in Chapter 45 that Joseph reaches a point of total forgiveness. There was no more torment. There was no more fear. Love had been perfected in him.

There were times when I had forgiven my father, but I still had iniquity towards him; however, God blessed me while there was iniquity in me towards him, because I controlled myself to the point of not acting on my thoughts.

In Psalm 18, David states God blessed him according to his righteousness, or his uprightness. He was found upright because *he kept himself* from iniquity, sinful thoughts and desires of the mind. Just because you feel resentment towards someone does not mean you are acting on that resentment. The first step to forgiveness is to choose not to react to what has been done. Because you are choosing to do something, this constitutes the fact that you are operating in love.

Why did God bless him despite the iniquity in his mind? Because God does not look at what your mind is thinking. He looks at what your heart is thinking. If God sees in your heart you are making continuous steps towards complete forgives He will continue to bless you and help you to achieve total forgiveness. However, if He sees the unforgiveness is in your heart He cannot bless you.

Now there are some people who can keep themselves from iniquity but they stop there. They never get to the next step, which is learning to live in love towards that person and destroying the iniquity. It is easy to forgive someone you are not in contact with, or have no close relations with, nor have any close relations with; however, a relative or someone you have constant contact with is the hardest to walk in love towards. Again, this is a decision.

A few people will learn to be cordial but they stop there. Complete forgiveness means you will do like Joseph did. (See Genesis 45:7.) When Joseph revealed himself to his brothers, he told them to go gather all their belongings and move to Egypt, so he could watch over their welfare. At this point, Joseph is truly operating in the Spirit of God, which is the Spirit of Love. There are degrees and levels of forgiveness and only when we get to the level of complete forgiveness are we *free*.

Our Ultimate Example

When we consider the pain and suffering Jesus went through, we cannot begin to compare ourselves. He was whipped with thirty-nine stripes. A crown of thorns was placed upon His head. He was hung on a Cross. They put nails in His hands and feet. They pierced Him in His side, and yet, for the very same men He died, saying, *"Father, forgive them for they know not what they do"* (Luke 23:34).

Philippians 2:8 states: *"And [Christ] being found in fashion as a man, he humbled himself, and became obedient unto death, even the death of the cross."*

I want you to think about this as we go into the next chapter. As children of God, Christ is our ultimate example. He did all this before we ever committed an offense. Forgiveness is readily available to us today. *What magnitude of forgiveness? What magnitude of love?*

The Rose that Blooms in Winter

In a field dressed in frosting white,
A rose, budding,
All by its lonesome.
What is this? One so daring
To dispute Mother Nature?
Who will triumph?

Day by day, I would come
To see, with this rose, what would be done.
In an environment of such a contrary degree,
The growth of the rose speaks of a mystery.

More and more, I see it bloom,
Yet wondering when its destruction would loom.
Intrigued by this rose's persistence to live,
This wonder, to me, it's joy would give.
It's fate would return me time and again,
And this very rose I would befriend.

On that day triumph in full blossom,
There stood the rose in such glory and splendor.
I rejoiced, shouting with a voice of victory.
There I would dance and there I would prance
With such glee and marvel at this rose's stance,
As if it were I that had overcome.

In a passionate red that would warm
the coldest heart.
With a fragrance so fresh, it stimulates the soul.
With petals so soft, reminiscent of the human touch.
How did she endure?

And now, God has used His gentle touch
To freeze this rose in the ice of time,
A legacy for generations to come.

1 Thessalonians 2:5-10

For neither at any time used we flattering words, as ye know, nor a cloke of covetousness; God is witness: Nor of men sought we glory, neither of you, nor yet of others, when we might have been burdensome, as the apostles of Christ. But we were gentle among you, even as a nurse [Mother]*cherisheth her children:

So being affectionately desirous of you, we were willing to have imparted unto you, not the gospel of God only, but also our own souls, because ye were dear unto us. For ye remember, brethren, our labour and travail: for labouring night and day, because we would not be chargeable unto any of you, we preached unto you the gospel of God. Ye are witnesses, and God also, how holily and justly and unblameably we behaved ourselves among you that believe:

* Emphasis added.

Chapter 8

A Mother's Love

The Marks of a Virtuous Woman

Words cannot express the love and appreciation I have for my mother. The things she did and the sacrifices she made are too many to mention. Yet, it is because of her love and her strength that I am who I am today. There have been many men who have helped me along the way but the love of God through my mother surpassed them all.

Strength to persevere, I learned from my mother. Taking the low road and being humble, I learned from my mother. Learning to forgive, I learned from my mother. Being a servant, I learned by the example of my mother. She is truly a unique and special person. She gave new light to the Scripture that says God will not put more on you than you can bear (1 Corinthians 10:13). Being stretched beyond her limits time and time again, she consistently overcame all obstacles and circumstances.

There were many times when my mother wanted to breakdown, but because of her love for my sister and me, she did not. She took her life and crucified it to a cross so we could have the best. There were many times she went without, so we would not. My mother is the most virtuous woman I have ever met or known. There are women who have done great things and are truly virtuous but there are none like my mother.

In Proverbs 31, King Lemuel discusses some of the wisdom and advice his mother gave him. The advice from a mother to a son is very beneficial, because how a young man interacts with his mother will carryover to how he interacts with other women. From our father's we learn to be protectors and providers, but from our mothers we learn to be caregivers and nurturers. Both parents are needed to provide balance in the lives of their children but as seen in my life, **a** *virtuous mother can be enough, even though it is not God's perfect will.*

Her Charge to Me

My mother literally dedicated her life to her children. Taking upon herself dual responsibilities, she raised us in the nurture and admonition of Jehovah God and Jesus Christ our Lord and Savior. I was her only male child and she was determined to raise me to be a man. She was not going to allow me to accept excuses as to why I could not do and be better. She pushed and challenged me to press past the limitations I had set for myself by believing lies that entered my mind saying *I wouldn't make it.* In her own words, *"I'm not going to raise no sorry man! It will not be said that a sorry excuse for a man came out of my womb! It will not be said!"*

As mentioned throughout this book, at the age of five my mother spoke words in my ears that would change my life forever. She said, *"From this day forward, you will have to be the man of the house."* As she was speaking, it seemed as if reality had suddenly slashed my back making my tiny hands lose their grip on a part of my life never to be retrieved.

As I began life's journey being led by a guide who had no idea how to show me my rite of passage, my mother and I struggled as we trickled through the trials booby trapped and woven into every man's walk of life.

In many of my trials, I had to be the strength and comforter of my mother. I gained my rite of passage to manhood through trial and error. With a guide not knowing what instructions to give me, there are still some walks of life I am not confident in. With a guide unsure of what path in which to lead me, there are some paths that are still undiscovered. A curious soul searching for a true light to follow, I wondered down some paths alone leading myself into unforeseen territory.

While being a self guide, my journey was deferred because of conflicting emotions. Searching desperately for a light to guide my life, I found myself following one light only to be intercepted by another light that appeared to seem more glamorous. However, no matter how glamorous, my soul's search was not fulfilled leading me back to where I started. My mother was neither happy nor mad because of my self-guided ventures, for there were some paths my mother was forbidden to travel, nor wanted to, but yet the road was destined for me.

As the years eroded away, my life became complicated by the evolution of more emotions. These feelings, when fulfilled gave me a false sense of completeness. During this time, I felt confident and secure. By this time in my life, I was venturing off from my mother, more often than not, searching to fulfill some part of my life. Time and time again I would find a missing piece to a puzzle only to find it did not fit the puzzle of my life.

So there I stood in life, confused, hurting, and searching for answers my mother could not provide. While these new feelings would momentarily ease my pain, after a limited stay within my heart, their departure made it harder than ever to deal with the pain. There were many times in my life when my mother did not have the answer*; however, my mother had something that was so much more powerful. Love.*

AGAPE

I remember while being in high school things got really tough for us financially. My mother did not care: she was going to do what it took to ensure her children were provided for. There were times when she would work two and three jobs to accomplish this goal. Her life was truly not her own and she made continual sacrifices to make sure we would have everything we needed (not wanted). When my sister was of age, she got a job because she wanted to be Miss Entrepreneur, but my mother would not let me get a job while I still lived in the house.

Her reason for doing so was she wanted me to focus on my studies. I could have gotten a job making minimum wage but my mother felt that was not enough to sacrifice for a good education, which would ensure me a better job in the future. I have heard of so many youths that had to get jobs because of their family's financial situation and a lot of them had to do so at the expense and sacrifice of their education; however, my mother would not let that be said of me.

I remember the period in time when my mother worked three jobs: all of them teaching positions. She would wake up in the morning at 6 A.M. so there would be enough time to make sure she, my sister, and I had enough time to get ready for school. During that time, she would cook breakfast, iron our clothes, and (for me) wake me up five or six times. At 7:30 A.M., we were all out of the door on our way to school. She was a high school teacher (imagine the stress) and worked this job until 3:30 P.M. She stayed later if there was a school activity for one of the clubs to which she was an advisor.

From there she would go to a local trade school and teach there for about two hours, from 4 to 6 P.M. After that class was over, she would rush home, cook dinner and eat. At 7:30 P.M., she would be out the door again to go teach at a night school, where people received their GED. She would be on this job until 10 P.M. After leaving there, she would come home and try to help me with my homework. Falling asleep, she would wake up only to do the same thing over and over again. She made herself a living sacrifice so my sister and I could have the best.

Shortly after my father left, my mother was diagnosed with breast cancer (I know her body broke down due to the stress and heartache of my father leaving). The doctor told her that she needed surgery. At that time, a patient stayed in the hospital after surgery under the doctor's care to make sure the proper healing occurs. I remember being in the room with her when she and the doctor had this conversation.

"Doctor, when will I be able to go home?"

"Well, Ms. Wilson, you have just come out of surgery. You are going to have to stay here so that we can monitor you."

Letting the doctor know his answer was not acceptable she replied, *"But who is going to take care of my children."*

My mother was not concerned with the circumstances. We were her responsibility and she wanted to ensure we were going to be taken care of. Even in her weakest moment, she exhibited strength. I know people who get caught up over the fact that they have a headache and they call in sick to work. My mother, on the other hand, insisted she was not staying in the hospital because she had work to do and children to raise. With the healing power of God working in her body, she was out of the hospital sooner than expected.

The only other person who has sacrificed so much for me in this life is Jesus Christ himself. My mother did not give her life for me as He did, but she did sacrifice it. Strength and honor are truly the clothing of my mother, and in time to come she shall rejoice. She shall rejoice because her prophecy came true. It will not be said that a sorry excuse for a man was born of her. I am going to make sure of that.

There were many people who offended my mother and our family. Yet, through it all, my mother did not slander them in front of us. In fact, she always found something positive to say about people and if there was not anything positive to say then she would just say, *"I'm not going to say anything at all."* She taught me humbleness and meekness (which I am still learning).

She continuously gave me examples of serving and blessing those who despitefully used her.

She even encouraged us to gain a relationship with our father. She did not try to keep us away from him, but would sometimes act as a mediator between us and him. There are so many mothers who use their children as a manipulative tool to either get back at the father or get even. My mother did neither, but she instilled in me the agape kind of love (unconditional). Despite what my father did she was not spiteful but continuously filled her mouth with the law of kindness.

My mother is a god-fearing woman. She was very involved in the church from the local level to the jurisdictional level. I am a third generation product of the Church of God in Christ. Growing up, we were members of Victory Temple COGIC (also known as Holy Ghost Headquarters), in Denmark, SC. There my mother held several positions, which included: church organist, minister of music, church secretary, Sunday school superintendent, teacher, YPWW moderator, and a missionary.

On the church district level, my mother was the district organist and choir member, district secretary, district Scholastic Motivational Ministries coordinator, and Youth department worker. On the jurisdictional level she held the following positions: Jurisdiction Scholastic Motivational Ministries coordinator, Youth department worker, Honors Club coordinator (in which she, herself, could not be nominated, due to the fact that it would be a conflict of interest, even though she spent countless hours working in the church to make sure that the house of God was taken care of), and choir member. My mother held so many positions it is impossible to remember them all.

Part of her responsibilities as the church and district secretary, included being the accountant for both. Despite the fact times were tough for us financially, not once was there a question about money missing from the offerings. Not only that, but in working with the youth department she did many of the activities at her own expense and far too many times she would do them without being paid for her services. However, being paid was not her heart.

Her heart was to take up the slack so the church could function. She was one of those persons who made other people look good. She did not look for glory, honor, or monetary reward: she only wanted to be pleasing unto God. Her love was for God, not man. That is why she would look past the faults of others and meet the needs of the people who needed her (this is another lesson I am still learning).

My mother is a servant at best. She held all of these positions simultaneously while working two and three jobs. Not once was it named something she did was a failure. She made sure of it and she made sure I was there to help make sure of it. My sister and I were mom's little helpers. We did not like it back then, but we appreciate it now.

The Development of Our Relationship

My mother was a busy person, needless to say. Because of that, we as a family did not get to know each other as well as we should have in the beginning. As time went on, conflict arose because of this. In speaking with God, I now understand my mother became real busy because as long as she did so she could keep her mind off of her hurt. However, while growing up neither I nor my sister, understood this.

She was a part of our lives as much as possible but there was a limit even to her. Many times when she would get sick it would be because her body was worn down. There were many times she was just too tired to do extra curricular activities with us. She had asthma, which restricted her activities. She also had allergies which restricted her outdoor activities. My mother was by no means perfect (who is); however, she did her best to be there for my sister and me, even though we did not think so at the time.

The relationship in our family was very mechanical. We were there playing the roles of a family, but the element of closeness was missing. There was the way my mother thought things should go. There was the way my sister thought things should go. And you better believe there was the way I thought things should go. We each began to play what I call the blame game. What we were doing was taking out our hurt on those that were closest to us.

This went on and on until one day while I was communing with God He spoke to me and said, *"I am trying my best to love you, but you won't let me."*

I said, "How, Lord?"

"Every time you reject the love of your mother, you are rejecting me. I am the one who gives her the strength to endure. I am the one who is holding her broken heart together. I am the one who is keeping her from falling apart. And as you have done unto her you have done unto me. When she feels like she can't make it she calls upon me to strengthen her. Just like my Son's thought of saving this dying world so does your mother think of providing for you a better life and it is me that gives her strength. You will respect her if you are to respect me."

During this time, my mother was her busiest, working three jobs as well as doing for the church. She surely did not need me rebelling against her because she was the one who stayed in my life. God made it plain if I was going to be blessed in this lifetime it would be because of how I treated my mother.

From that time forward, I began to change my attitude towards my mother. My mother used to cook in between jobs to make sure I ate. I would get home from school around 4 P.M. and essentially only had homework to do. My mother came in around 6 P.M. to cook. Soon after I received that revelation from God I began to have a meal prepared for my mother when she came home. I started off by cooking hot dogs and macaroni and cheese. Later, I called my grandmother to find out what ingredients I needed in order to cook different kinds of meals. After all, my mother deserved steak. She deserved the best.

I began to do things that would help her get some rest. I began to learn how to take the load off of her. The things I did were small, but my heart was in it. I was beginning to come into the measure of what a man should do. A man should be there to take the load off of the woman.

First Peter 3:7 says women should be *honored* as the weaker vessel, not because they are the weaker vessel. My mother proved that to be true. Yet, she still deserved to be honored and I was going to be the man to do it. I was beginning to become the man my mother wanted me to be. Not only was I becoming responsible, but I was beginning to see the needs of others and help meet those responsibilities as well.

Even though I began to do these things, our relationship still was not what I wanted it to be. There was still an element missing. Of course we got closer, but that mother-son relationship was not quite there yet. It did not really begin to develop until I did one of the simplest, yet convicting things I could have ever done. I told her, *"I Love You."*

I remember the first time I did. She was coming home from her second job. Now sometimes when she would come home I would cut off all the lights and hide from her. I would wait until the right moment and jump out in front of her and yell, *"Aarrh,"* as if I were a monster. She *really* did not like me doing that. But this day was different. She came home and opened the door. As soon as she walked in, I came up to her, gave her a hug, and said, *"Mom, I love you."*

Right there in my arms she broke down and cried. Those words alone opened the door that had been closed for so long. I do not remember ever telling my mother I loved her until I was in high school. We had gone so long without saying it that it was not a part of our daily routine. Love was something that was implied and not said. I broke the silence and from that day forward I made a conscious decision to tell her I loved her on a consistent basis.

I also began to do other things for her that would make her smile, and sometimes embarrass her. We would be at home and I would sit down on her lap as if I were a little kid. I would, at the same time, act as a little kid. That really aggravated her, but I knew it also made her feel loved. I would sometimes sit beside her and lay my head on her shoulder while she was busy. She would tell me I was getting on her nerves but I could tell by the smile on her face it did not bother her too much. My mother was very time oriented and I would do things purposely to throw a wrench in her gears so she would take her mind off of work if but for a second.

In public is where I really embarrassed my mother. I would see her at a distance and would yell, *"Hey good looking, what you got cooking."* I would pretend as if she was my girlfriend, which she did not like, but I got a kick out of it. Sometimes I would go up to hug her and pick her up off the ground. Hey, she was only 5' 1" and I was 5' 11". I figured I needed to bring her up to my level. Needless to say, she did not like that either. It was not so much that she did not like it as much as the fact that it embarrassed her. That did not matter to me; I wanted her to know she had my attention and my affection.

If affection is not a part of our families, then we have nothing more than roommates. Affection is love in emotion; those things you do to evoke your love within the other person. It can be done by doing the simplest things. A hug, a kiss, or as I did, simply embarrass the person in a way that shows the world you love them and they are appreciated. Affection, or the lack thereof, will determine what kind of relationship your family will have.

We did not have everything, but when we gained affection we did. Now, there is not a time that goes by I do not tell my mother I love her. She is more than a mother, she is a friend. Now whenever we call each other, we greet one another by saying, *"Wassup."* I remember talking to her on my cell phone one day and I greeted her as such. When the call was ended, I said, *"I love you, mom"* and the friend I was with looked at me as if I was crazy.

"You talk to your mom that way?"

"Yeah, we got it like that," because we do.

Becoming a Man

Genesis 2:24a states: *"Therefore shall a man leave his father and his mother...."*

A day that was destined to come came all too soon for my mother. I was entering manhood and more and more making my own decisions. I was beginning to branch out as a young man should do. I was growing up and that posed some problems at first because she felt she was losing me. She will never lose me. I will always be a momma's boy and she will always be the love of my life. Even now that I am married, my mother will still be a part of my life. I am going to bless her tremendously for what she has done for me.

However, my breaking off from my mother was very hard for both of us. I was, and am, her baby boy. She had dedicated her entire life to helping me to get to this point, and when we got there it was hard to let go. There is a special bond between my mother and me that will never be broken. To this day, she still has a card I made for her when I was in elementary school.

Yet, there came a day when I began to make decisions she did not necessarily approve of. My decision making made her feel as if she was no longer needed in my life, which was the farthest thing from the truth. I still needed her in my life but in a different way. I needed to break away if I was to become the man she truly wanted me to be. She raised me to be a man of God and when I began to go after things I knew God wanted me to do, she did not like it. Not because she did not want me to move towards God, but because she saw me moving away from her.

After a period of time, she began to understand I will always be her baby boy forever, no matter where I am, or who I become in the eyes of society. She truly knows I love her and I will always be there for her. After all, she is the one who nurtured me, clothed me, and gave me shelter. I learned a lot about what a man should do for his family by watching her. Everything else, I had to learn on my own. I made some mistakes, but my mother taught me how to take responsibility whenever a mistake is made.

I am becoming the man she raised me to be. Her prophecy over my life will come to pass and I will do great things for my God in Jesus' name and authority. There are many things I desire to do and have. The greatest of my desires is to have a family so I can show my mother she did not raise a sorry excuse for a man, nor will it be said that out of her womb came such a man. Her words will not lie. I will be sure of that.

Mom, I love you more than words can say and I dedicate the rest of my life to being the man of God you raised me to be.

Psalm 115:11-14

Ye that fear the LORD, trust in the LORD:
he is their help and their shield.
The LORD hath been mindful of us: he will bless us;
he will bless the house of Israel;
he will bless the house of Aaron.
He will bless them that fear the LORD,
both small and great.
The LORD shall increase you more and more, you and your children.*

*[Author emphasis due to special personal meaning.]

Chapter 9

We Still Need Our Fathers

You Are Our Glory

As a father, you are very much needed in their lives. Your presence alone helps to give them confidence and stability. With the slightest bit of involvement, they appreciate what you do. As children, they take pride in who their father is because they are born into this world connected by their hearts. Children are born loving their fathers.

Their fathers are their glory. The word glory is translated from the Hebrew word *tiph'arah*, which means beauty, splendor, glory, renown, honor, and boast. Do you see that? You are their glory, their honor. They make their boast in you. In Psalm 34:2, the psalmist states he will make his boast in the Lord. He makes this claim because of who God has proven himself to be in his life. Likewise, children love to boast about what their father is to them. The only problem is they cannot make a boast if there is nothing to boast about.

In talking with some of my friends, they would tell me how their fathers would take them fishing and how many fish they brought home. They would give detail about how their fathers would take the time to teach them the ins and outs of fishing. After their expedition, they would scale the fish, gut it out, cook it, and eat the fruit of their labor. The mistakes they made were often sources of immediate laughter, but the memories were everlasting.

I had other friends whose fathers taught them how to drive. Some even worked on the car with their fathers, learning a trade. One after another, they would make their boast in what their fathers taught them. This tells me that as children they want you to teach them. They are watching you and earnestly gleaning from your every move.

Train up (Proverbs 22:6). The Hebrew word for train is *"chanakh,"* which means to initiate, teach, dedicate, consecrate and inaugurate.

Fathers are to initiate the development of the child along the correct path teaching them responsibility and accountability. Fathers are to teach by word and deed. Whether you know it or not, you are teaching them. Now whether they are being well trained or badly trained depends on what they do. As proven in a previous chapter, the faults of the father are most often duplicated by the child. As our parent, you are supposed to train your children up in the way they *should go*; however, too many times they are trained to go the wrong way.

Children need you to take responsibility in your life because it will give them responsibility in theirs. You may have made a mistake, but by correcting it they will learn to correct theirs too. They pattern themselves after you. When they get in situations they have never faced before and are there by themselves, they think, *what would my parents do,* and in many cases, the parent they think of is their father. Why? Because they learn from you.

Furthermore, fathers are to dedicate their children. When something is dedicated it is set aside for a special use. It is also carefully guarded, so that which is dedicated will not be used outside of its intended purpose. In order for a father to do this, he must be there to protect his children. We live in a loose world and the elements of it are tantalizing and tempting. If not taught correctly, children will end up indulging in things that are detrimental to their lives.

Something dedicated is considered to be *holy*, and that is what children are. And if children are holy, then that makes their fathers priests, because only priests are allowed to handle that which is dedicated unto God and set apart as holy. Fathers are responsible for making sure that their children grow up to fulfill their intended use.

A part of fathers fulfilling that obligation is also to consecrate their children. To consecrate means to make hallow. When you hallow something, you purge it from filth and impurities. You clean it up and prepare it for its intended use. Too many times parents groom their children outwardly with the appropriate clothing to be accepted in certain settings without grooming them inwardly with the appropriate character as well.

Children should be dedicated (set apart) for an intended use and also consecrated (prepared) for that intended use. However, too many times they enter into society not prepared to handle the woes of this world, so they end up doing what they want. If they are consecrated and dedicated, then they will know what their life's purpose is. And when the temptations of this world come to get them off track, they will still succeed because they will know who they are.

They will know who they are because they will be inaugurated. To inaugurate means to induct into office in a formal manner. As a father, it is your responsibility to declare to your children, who they are. Furthermore, this declaration should occur before all. It should be made known that they are your children, and that as such, they have all the rights and privileges that come along with being so.

To inaugurate also means to set in motion. In life there are many stages we go through. A father's job is to set their children's lives in motion along the right path at each stage they come to. At the beginning of each stage, the father should be there to give instructions, prepare them for possible temptations, and send them off with a head start.

1 Thessalonians 2:11 states: *"As ye know how we exhorted and comforted and charged every one of you, as a father doth his children."*

A father's job is also to *exhort, comfort and charge* his children (I Thessalonians 2:11). This tells just how important a father is in the development of a child. However, to get a better understanding of this verse let us look at each of the bold print words.

Exhort. To exhort means to admonish, this simply means to build up. Fathers have a great deal of influence when it comes to building the esteem and character of their children. In a previous chapter, it was noted the children who live in single-parent households, where the father is the guardian, exhibit similar behavioral patterns as those who were raised in dual-parent households.

The encouragement of a father goes beyond what words can say. I remember when I would tell my father something I did and he would say, *"Alright."* Just those words alone would make me stick my ribcage out and place a smile on my face. My father was proud of me which gave me something to be proud about. It encouraged me to do better, to keep going on and continue to chase my dreams. All because he said one word. *Oh, how great is the influence of our fathers.*

Comfort. To comfort means to console in a time of grief. God, as our Heavenly Father, told us we should cast our cares upon Him (1 Peter 5:7). He told us this because He cares for us so much He does not want us to be burdened down with any worries. Likewise, natural fathers should be there so they can come to them and find consolation when they feel overburdened.

There will be times when life will deal us one too many blows at the same time. There will be times when temptation arises on every side. There will be times in life when we miss it and make mistakes. There will be times when we place ourselves in dire positions. In these times, we feel as if we are failures and without some one there to comfort us and exhort us to get back up and finish our course, we will become too discouraged to go forward. As feminine as it may sound, we need our fathers to be our greatest cheerleaders.

Charge. As a father, it is your duty to charge your children, to implore and beseech them to succeed. In those times when your children feel like they cannot make it up the hills of life, it is your responsibility to give them that boost they need to make it. You have the ability to boost and charge up their confidence because they know you are not going to let them fail.

When they say we cannot seem to make it, you should be there to say, *"Yes you can."* When they say it is too hard, you should be there to say, *"You can do all things through Christ because you are an overcomer."* When they feel they cannot do it alone, you should be there to say, *"I'll never leave you nor forsake you."* And in those times when they feel they are losing the battle of life, you should be the one telling them to *"Fight the good fight of faith."* Charge them to move forward and onward as good soldiers enduring this battle.

Satan Despises Fathers

They are your children and they need you more than you could ever know. They know that. God knows that. And the Devil knows that too. He knows fathers represent God to their children. He knows a father is one of the main vessels through whom God can flow blessings into the life of a child. The Devil knows this and he hates it.

Children, look and search so desperately to find someone to give them their spirit of approval. Because the Devil knows this he sends people into their path to approve of them and get them on the wrong path. By nature, we, being human, look for acceptance. We will turn our hearts towards anyone who will give it to us, even those who mean us no good. When children have the acceptance of their fathers, the strength of peer pressure is not so great. On the other hand, when they do not have the approval of their fathers they look elsewhere.

Even for those who have their fathers in their lives, if their father does not give them approval they will become disheartened. There are children who live with their fathers, but their father is the source of contention in their lives. Because we are human, we make mistakes. As a father, one must have wisdom in how to address the mistakes of their children.

A father who does not know how to do this will drive a wedge between him and his children. The way a father answers his child will either build that child up or tear that child down. There are two verses in the Bible that speak to parents provoking there children, Colossians 3:21 and Ephesians 6:4, *both of which are addressed to fathers.*

There are many fathers who do not know how to speak to their children (Proverbs 15:1). Whenever they do something wrong, they come down on them in condemnation. A father is very much needed to build and edify the child. This will not happen if the father is constantly putting the child down. Grievous words from a father to a child can do a lot more damage than can be said. There are some children who will cry even if they think they have let their parents down.

The harsh words of a father can and will produce discouragement in a child. They will feel worthless, because to their father they just cannot seem to do anything right. The moment they encounter someone who makes them feel as if they have done something right, they will attach themselves to that person. They need love and acceptance from their fathers.

If they do not get it from you, the Devil will send out his wolves in sheep's clothing to prey on their lives. The Devil wants to divide the fathers from their children because fathers represent the image of God. He wants our families divided.

When the Devil came to Adam and Eve as a serpent, he deceived Eve into thinking if she ate the fruit of the Tree of Knowledge of Good and Evil she would be *more* like her Father, Jehovah. His whole ploy was that God was trying to keep them from being like Him, as if He was trying to keep them from enjoying something He was. Likewise, today, many children fall to peer pressure because people make them feel as if their parents are trying to keep them from something.

Now of course, God disciplined Adam and Eve for what they did, and fathers should likewise discipline their children. However, after God disciplined Adam and Eve, He turned around and gave them clothes. In other words, He helped them to understand there were consequences for their actions, but even though they made a mistake He helped them make the best of things.

He did not leave them naked, even though it was because of their own doing as to why they were that way. This is the pattern every father should follow. As stated, children will make mistakes, but a father is supposed to be a shelter, which is a place of refuge. That is what God is and He is our heavenly Father. If fathers would only pattern themselves after the ultimate example, what kind of society would we have? You are already in the image of God (that is why the Devil hates you); allow your character to be in His likeness.

Someone Offended Can Be Won Over

It is hard to win someone over whom you have offended. Some of the greatest relationships are destroyed because of offense. In the Bible, Paul and Barnabas had so much tension between them they had to part ways (Acts 15:36-41). The whole ordeal was over the fact Paul did not want John Mark to accompany them on the mission. Valid reason or not, this caused two friends who entered into the ministry together to separate. Division is never God's plan.

Still, it is hard to win an offended brother over. However, nowhere in the Bible does it signify winning someone over who has been offended is impossible, just hard. In order to do so, you have to somehow prove yourself valuable to that person. In the example given, Paul is later reconciled with Mark, for he tells Timothy to bring Mark with him when he comes because he is now profitable to Paul (2 Timothy 4:11) and he tells the Colossians to accept Mark if he comes to them (Colossians 4:10). This proves that they can be won over, but the question is, *"How hard are you willing to try to win them over?"*

Many times by your actions or your words, both fathers and mothers tear down their child's self-esteem. In doing so, the child becomes offended and begins to erect walls. This is especially true when a divorce occurs. The parent loses the trust of the child and they are wondering why the relationship between them and their child is strained. Can things change? Yeah, but you have to be the one to make sure that it does. Remember, you are the initiator.

What you must understand is you have offended the child. There is a big part of the child that does not want anything to do with you. You also must understand nothing is in your favor at this point. However, I want you to know this is just a ploy by the child to see if you really care. If the child can run you away because it is too tough to get close to him or her, then they also believe you will run away again when times get tough. They do not want someone who is in and out of their lives, so if you run into some hard times at first you should understand why.

You have to allow the child to grant you access into their world. In their world are many doors to many rooms. While developing the relationship there may be some doors the child will open immediately while others will take longer. This is because there will be boundaries established by the child. If you abide by these boundaries respect will develop between you and the child. If you do not respect these boundaries you could end up pushing the child farther away. When this happens the doors that were open to you will become closed again.

As a father, they are looking for you to take the first step. You were the one that left so you should be the one to return. Furthermore, God gave them to you; therefore, it is your responsibility to take them under your wings, not wait until they come to you and ask you to. When you left you essentially said you did not want to take the responsibility for them. You were the one who abandoned them, not vice versa.

The children may want and desire a relationship, but they are not going to run after you. Their thought pattern is saying, *"If he loves me, he will come for me. He will take the initiative to re-establish the relationship."* By not doing anything you signify to them you are not willing to reestablish the covenant. Even though an explanation is not given, the one ascribed is you do not want it.

You may say you do not have the time you wish you had to reestablish the relationship, but to them that says you do not want to find the time. As children, they believe you will make time for something that is important to you. The amount of time you place into developing a relationship with them will signify how important they are to you.

Apologize. You may be wondering what is the first thing you should do. Do something you and the child loved when you were together. Good times are always a good way to rekindle any dying flame. Allow the child to open up to you and when you feel they are open, apologize. You will be surprised at how far these words can carry the relationship.

It tells the child you acknowledge the problems in the relationship are because of you. In apologizing, do not, I repeat, do not try to offer an excuse for not being there. I do not care what excuse you use, it will not be accepted. Furthermore, that child will feel as if you are just there as a means of self-justification. You may not have liked their mother, in-laws, etc., or whatever, but that child feels your love for them should be greater than your hatred towards anyone else.

Showing the child you are willing to take total responsibility for your actions will also teach them to do the same. If children see you feel that you do not have to apologize for your mistakes then they will feel the same. Furthermore, it shows them you do not think enough of them to apologize. This is pride, which is the opposite of humility. By apologizing, you are showing them you are willing to prefer their feelings above your ego.

A Gift. This is really not a good idea. Most people feel money is the solve-all and end-all. Trust me, it is not. If you come to your child bearing gifts, they will accept your gifts and still reject you. They cannot be bought. It tells them your not being there can be substituted with a price; however, you cannot place a price on time, memories and love.

This is one mistake my father made. He felt that he could buy his way back into my life. He would ask me what I wanted and I would tell him something that cost an astronomical price. Why? It would have only been a down payment for the time lost. Of course, I never got it. Really, I never expected to.

Other times, he would ask me what I wanted and I would tell him that I did not want anything. There are some things in life you cannot place a monetary value on. I did not want him to get the idea that showering me with gifts would be acceptable for what he did. I did not want him to feel vindicated by the gift he gave. At one point, my feelings were that I did not want anything from him at all and my life would be better off without him.

I am not saying to not give a gift. Gifts are another way of causing a closed door to be opened. They have the ability to smooth out any tension that may be there. It is good as a short-term solution. In giving the gift, you may want to explain the gift in no way is a payoff for what has happened in the past.

You want to give the explanation because if you do not the child may hold you to giving them gifts every time you get together. You cannot pay the debt you owe for not being there and if you try, that child will be expecting you to pay it for the rest of your life (and you would still have a balance owed). If you start giving gifts and you stop, you are back at square one.

By initiating the relationship with a gift, you are saying, *"This is how I am going to repay you."* By stopping, you can send a message to the child that you have started something and now you are stopping. This will make them think you no longer care about them. What you do to start a relationship is what you will need to do to keep it going.

Like I said, a gift will open the door but it means nothing if you do not follow through. Without following through, this too is conveying the thought that you feel money is an acceptable substitute for what you did. Guess what? It is not and if you do not understand this you will never have a decent relationship with your child.

Promises. Promises. Promises. Do not make them if you cannot keep them. This will only put you deeper into the hole than you already are. Children, we do not need to be put through emotional roller coasters. Making a promise and not keeping it causes you to lose credibility. Furthermore, you risk the chance of further wounding the child depending upon what you promise.

One promise my father made me was he was going to come back for me and take me with him. Well, that became my hope. I waited and waited for his return much the same way that the church now awaits Christ's immediate return. Days turned into months, and months into years, and soon a living hope of my father coming to get me became a dying dream. He never came back to take me with him.

There were other promises that were changed at the last minute. It got to the point where I no longer got excited when he told me something. You see making promises is a good way of building hope but coming through on them validates you. Like my father, others do it as a way of trying to bridge a relationship; trying to prove their worth. A promise not kept can do more damage than not making a promise at all.

By not making a promise, it may take the relationship longer to develop, but at least the things you do will be appreciated. Instead of making a null promise, just surprise the child from time to time. When they receive something unexpected, it will make them think you were thinking about them. A promise can only be made when the two of you are together; however, a surprise means you were thinking of them while you were apart. This will cause you to gain ground.

Start where they are. Please realize the relationship may not start where it ended. Since then the child has grown, matured and changed. There will be some things that are different about them. Find out how they have changed and do not treat them as if they are still the same as they were before you left.

Your first steps should be finding out who the child is now and go from there. Old interests may not be there anymore, but new ones can always be made. Find out their dreams and do what you can to help them achieve them. Get to know them and love them for who they are. If they are not who you want them to be, just remember you were not there to help guide them.

The best thing you could do is to show them you love them and you appreciate them for who they are. This will develop a trust between you and them. Most of all, it will cause them to appreciate you. They will feel you are interested in the direction their life is going and they will invite you into their life a little further.

One of the worst things that you could do is to treat a teenager as if he or she is still in grade school. The older a child gets the more respect they will require from you, especially if you have not been there. Take time to find out who the new *he or she* is. Find out what is going on in their lives, and learn to compliment the positive.

Dealing with the negative may not be such a good idea at first. This is because to them you have no authority or right to say anything to them in such cases. Build the relationship first and then address the negative at a later time. Remember, your right to express your opinion left the same day you did, and you will be treated as such.

If you think the problem needs to be addressed immediately then address it through their guardian(s). Talk it over with them because the child is living in their house. If they do not see anything wrong with it, then you leave it alone. It may be a matter of opinion or maybe not. Just because you are the daddy does not give you the privilege to interject your say-so if you have not been there. That is a privilege of a father.

Yes, you may have a valid point and the guardian, who is usually the mother, may not want to address it simply because you brought it up. However, that is something you should address with them, not the child. Do not do anything with the child that would hinder the relationship from going forward. Please understand, even though you are not addressing the negative does not mean you have to approve of it. It just means you should address it through someone else until you have been given that authority from the child.

Also, remember you are not that child's guardian. Do not try to usurp their guardian's authority. What some parents who are not in the household do to gain popularity is to allow the child freedom their guardians will not. By doing this you drive enmity between the child and their legal guardians. You are coming into the child's life to help and edify the child. However, you must understand one of your roles and responsibilities is to help *reinforce* the values their guardian has instilled in them. If you do not like the values that the child has, remember this: a large part of the blame lies on your shoulders because you left. Furthermore, it is hard to change something from the outside. Gain their trust first and then you can help bring about change.

Wait until you have established a relationship with the child and the guardian before addressing any negatives. The guardians have a right to address any problem they may see, you do not. Doing these things will not only show the child you want to be a part of their life, but it will also show the guardians that you can be trusted to be a part of their life, and they (both the child and the guardians) will appreciate you for that.

So go. Call your children and let them know that even though you've made a mistake by not being there, they are still very precious to you. Don't just tell them. Show them.

Still Longing for My Father

It is my prayer this book ministers to both fathers and their children. I pray God begins to turn the hearts of the fathers towards the sons and the hearts of the sons towards the fathers. I pray this book will reach unto the utter most part of this Earth. However, I would give anything to not have had the experience and knowledge to write this book. No amount of money in the world could ever compare to the joy I had when my father was in my life when I was a small child.

I thank God for using me to write this book. It is one that is very much needed because this issue needs to be addressed. I only wish this book was written about 50 years ago so that my father could have been ministered to. Had my father understood this information when he was growing up I would never have had to learn it. I am not bitter about my life and I made the very best of it but I would be lying to say I do not even care my father was not there.

As I now look over my father's life and some of the decisions that he made, I can truly say that my father did not do what he did out of spite or hatred. However, like most men, my father masked his internal emotions so that the world would not see his pain. When men do this, they make mistakes that they will surely regret at a later time. My father loves me and I love him. And even though our relationship was not what it should have been, we are now making every effort to help it become what it should be.

As with any relationship, there are times when we do not see eye to eye, but even then, I know that he loves me. It has long been my prayer that God restore my relationship with my natural father and I can truly say that God is now answering my prayer. I now understand that part of what I went through was so that God's glory could be revealed on my behalf; and not only my behalf, but on the behalf of everyone who desires to rekindle their relationship, to know their father and to be a father.

God promised restoration in our families and now is the time for God's promise to be fulfilled.

Malachi 4:5, 6 states: *"Behold, I will send you Elijah the prophet before the coming of the great and dreadful day of the LORD: And he shall turn the heart of the fathers to the children, and the heart of the children to their fathers, lest I come and smite the earth with a curse."*

In closing, please pray this prayer as I join my faith with yours concerning this issue:

Dear heavenly Father: I thank you for who you have been to me. Thank you for being the father I did not have. Thanks for shielding me and protecting me from attacks of the enemy that I did not even know were heading my way. Thank you for bringing me through every trial and tribulation the Devil has brought against me.

Lord God, I believe your word and I believe your promises, and I thank you that you are going to restore my relationship with my father/child(ren). It is your desire that we be together, for it was you who placed us into each other's life. Give us wisdom and love to build the kind of relationship that you have always desired for us to have.

I thank you for answering this prayer, in Jesus' name. Amen.

Now that you have prayed this prayer, pray it again and again and again until the relationship you desire is made a reality. May God sincerely bless you and may your broken relationship be restored in Jesus' name. God Bless.

An Invitation to Know the "Father" of all Fathers

Psalm 27:10 states: *"When my father and my mother forsake me, then the LORD will take me up."*

So many people are looking for refuge in a father, and for whatever reason, it has not happened yet. Well, I have some good news for you. The LORD is willing to take up the slack where your father has left off. Or maybe you are a father reading this book and you realize the mistakes you made. God is faithful and just to forgive you. In either case, God wants to change your life.

I pray something you read ministered to your spirit just as it did for me even while I was writing it. Yet, I offer you the chance to get to know the one who can minister to you on a personal level. I invite you to know Jesus Christ as your Lord and Savior. Let Him take your life and start it afresh. I guarantee your end will be *victorious!*

Just say this following prayer:

Father, God, Creator of us all, I thank you for sending your Son, Jesus Christ, to die for me. I repent of my sins and I confess Jesus as Lord of my life. I believe that He died for me and on the third day, He arose out of the grave. I believe with all my hear t that by His grace, I am saved. In Jesus' Name, Amen.

Guess what. Just like that, you are a child of the King. What does that mean now? Where do you go from here? Allow God to lead you in the direction you should go. Talk to Him in prayer and quiet your soul to hear His voice. If you are not a member of a local church, then allow Him to lead you where He would like you to fellowship.

If you are a member of a church, get involved. Show Him you love Him. He is not asking you to be perfect. He is only asking you to acknowledge Him in everything you do, and He will direct your path. (See Proverbs 3:6.) Allow yourself to become a son of the living God.

May God richly bless you, in Jesus' name!

Special Acknowledgements

Special thanks to the following:

Jesus Christ—It is because of your death, burial and resurrection that I am accepted as a son of the Most High God.

Mom—your unyielding love, though tough, helped to shape me into the man that I am toady.

Grandma—your prayers, your Bible studies and your sweet potato pie ... what can I say except, I love you!

Dad—I truly look forward to the relationship that God is now allowing us to build.

Bishop Keith A. Butler—Thank you for the teaching, instructions and principles of faith I received from the Word of Faith.

Bishop Wayne T. & Dr. Beverly Y. Jackson—Thank you for your personal prayers and your personal faith on my behalf. Your love is greatly appreciated. The blessing is truly stronger than the curse.

Pastors Herbert & Marcia Bailey—Thank you for carrying me on your backs as I struggled through my transition in life. The unconditional love you have shown me makes me feel like a son—I love you both.

Karen—The love that you have brought to my life far exceeded my expectations. I truly look forward to the future that we have already begun with each other on April 9, 2005. I pray to God continuously that He teaches me to be the husband you need and the father our family will need.

Dennis—To my beloved son, you just don't know how proud I am of you and how much I love you. You have greatness on the inside of you and one day you are going to make both your mother and me proud.

Contact and Ordering Information

If this book has been a blessing to your life in some way, we would love to hear from you. Or, maybe you would like Terrence to be a keynote speaker for an event. If so, please visit his website for more contact information: www.wilstonian.com

Bless someone with a copy of *In Search of a Father* today

Additional Resources Available:

Project Timothy—If you are looking for to either start a mentoring program or be a part of one, please visit us at www.wilstonian.com/Project-Timothy/main.htm.

Here you will be able to listen to audio files and download mentorship material so that you can follow along. This is available to everyone, whether formalized mentorship programs, youth groups, and even single mothers...

We pray it will bless you on the road to manhood.